ARTISANS for INDEPENDENCE

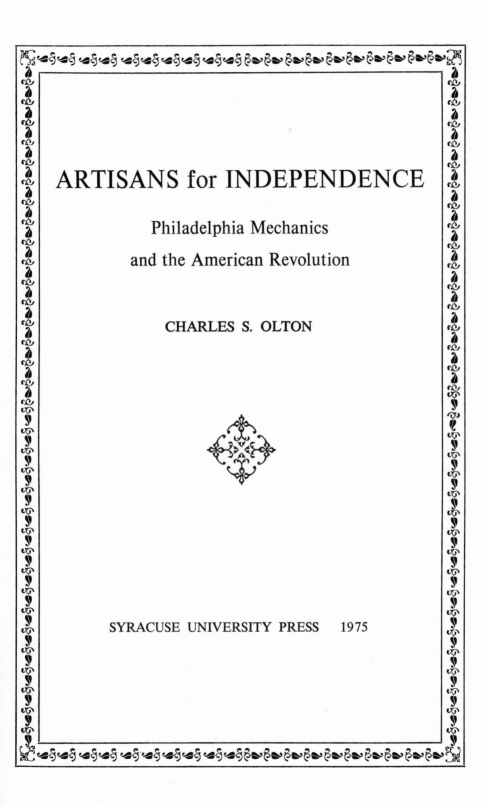

ARTISANS for INDEPENDENCE

Philadelphia Mechanics
and the American Revolution

CHARLES S. OLTON

SYRACUSE UNIVERSITY PRESS   1975

Library of Congress Cataloging in Publication Data

Olton, Charles S   1938–
    Artisans for independence.

    Bibliography: p.
    Includes index.
    1.   Artisans—Philadephia—Political activity—
    History.   I.   Title.
HD2346.U52P56   322.4'2'0974811   75-23003
ISBN 0-8156-0111-5

Manufactured in the United States of America

For Barbara

Charles S. Olton, associate professor of history at the State University of New York College at Buffalo, is the author of a number of articles on the history of the American Revolution. He has also been an academic administrator at Union College and at Buffalo.

Contents

Preface

THIS BOOK BEGAN as an attempt to carry forward into the era of the American Revolution a history of urban artisans begun by Carl Bridenbaugh in *The Colonial Craftsman*. It quickly became apparent, however, that the kind of general history of artisans and craftsmen which had been written about the earlier Colonial period would not be possible for the Revolutionary years. The elaborate and extensive network of political, social, and economic histories of this period, as well as the substantial variations in the histories of the several major manufacturing centers, would require more comprehensive treatment of the subject than the then current level of historical knowledge would allow. Not even the initial spadework had begun on the study of the common man in America during the Revolution.

A choice was therefore made to write a case study—to analyze the artisans of one city in detail and to define the scope of the peoples under scrutiny rather sharply, in the hope that what could be said of one city might be transferrable, at least in part, to other urban centers, and in the further hope that a study limited to the most aggressive and active segment of the city's lower social echelons would become a springboard for later and larger generalizations about the common man in urban America. This book, then, is a case study of Philadelphia's artisans and mechanics—the city's independent *master* craftsmen—during the period from 1765 to 1790.

The city of Philadelphia was chosen not because it was typical (there was no such thing in eighteenth-century America), but because it was the biggest city, the most modern city, the most dynamic city, and the city with the most useful records for the purposes of this investigation. Although many of the conclusions which may be reached from an analysis of Philadelphia are peculiar to that city, there are some generalizations which go beyond. Studies of Charleston and New York by Richard Walch and Staughton Lynd indicate that some of the conclusions reached here about Philadelphia may apply to those cities, as well. Boston's Revolutionary mechanics have yet to be studied.

More important than restricting this study to the history of a single city was the decision to define the subject—the artisans and craftsmen—fairly narrowly. All students of eighteenth-century America have experienced frustration in trying to understand social classes: they were ill-defined and mercurial in composition, and yet they existed and clearly were important to Colonial society. The artisans were also called tradesmen, craftsmen, and mechanics. One is never sure whether the terms were purposely or only accidentally used synonymously in eighteenth-century parlance; nor can one say with confidence who was, and who was not, included within the group, however it was then defined.

The decision to restrict the definition of the subject (which is explained and justified in the second chapter) to master mechanics who were independent entrepreneurs had a major impact on this book's results and conclusions. Inasmuch as artisans and mechanics (as herein defined) were not part of the segment of society to which political, economic, and social leadership were traditionally deferred, their story represents a part of the recent attempt to comprehend American history "from the bottom up." But the "bottom" is a bourgeoisie, not a proletariat. Although there were dependent laboring people in eighteenth-century American cities, they did not have nearly as much influence on the development of urban Revolutionary history as did middle-class people who wore the leather apron. Nearly everyone in urban America was involved in the effort to determine "who should rule at home," but it was the middle-class artisans and mechanics who outlined the objectives, set the pace, provided the leadership, and reaped the benefits of the Revolutionary turmoil. Until we understand their story, the story of other "meaner" or "inferior" urban Americans of the Revolution will not become clear.

In short, this book is only a beginning. It represents a piece of the story of the lower social orders, the common men, the mobs, the laboring classes, the "inarticulate" who affected so much of our Revolutionary history. Much yet remains to be done.

I owe thanks to many, without whose encouragement and assistance this book would not have been written. My interest in eighteenth-century urban social history was first stimulated by Carl Bridenbaugh's graduate seminar at Berkeley many years ago. It was sustained by my dissertation mentor, Robert Middlekauff, who both challenged me to think rigorously and demanded that my work come to terms with existing scholarship. As the study moved through several revisions, I benefited greatly from the knowledge and enthusiasm of many friends and colleagues who generously shared their own scholarship and who read and criticized drafts of the manuscript. Mentioning their names is not thanks enough: John K. Alexander, of the University of Cincinnati; Peter J. Parker, of the Historical Society of Pennsylvania; Roger W. Moss, Jr., of the Athenaeum of Philadelphia; Merrill Jensen, of the University of Wisconsin; Owen Stephen Ireland, of the State University of New York College at Brockport; Hannah Roach, of the Historical Society of Pennsylvania; and my colleagues at Union College. A great deal of thanks goes to Alfred Young, of Northern Illinois University, who offered detailed and thoughtful criticism of several drafts and who kept after me to see the work through to publication. His interest in the field of the history of the urban common man is, and will remain, the inspiration of many young historians and the catalyst of a fresh approach to the history of the American Revolution. Of course neither he nor the others I have mentioned may be considered responsible for errors of fact or interpretation in this book.

I wish also to thank several libraries which have made their resources available to me and which have permitted me to quote from documents and manuscripts in their possession. These include the Historical Society of Pennsylvania, the Library of Congress, the New York Public Library, the American Philosophical Society, the Library Company of Philadelphia, the Carpenters' Company, the Friends Historical Library at Swarthmore College, the Henry Francis du Pont Winterthur Museum, and the libraries of Union College, the University of California at Berkeley, and Swarthmore College. My research was supported by several small grants from Union College and the University of California at Berkeley.

Most of all, I owe thanks to my wife, Barbara K. Olton. She and my children have endured me and the Philadelphia artisans for an unreasonably long time, and for their perseverance I shall be eternally grateful.

Charles S. Olton

Buffalo, New York
Spring 1975

ARTISANS for INDEPENDENCE

On the Eve of Revolution

"**Y**OU will consider Philadelphia," Robert Morris once wrote to John Hancock, "from its centrical situation, the extent of its commerce, the number of its artificers, manufacturers and other circumstances, to be to the United States what the heart is to the human body in circulating the blood."[1] The assertion was not merely Morris' chauvinism. Philadelphia was the leading city in America at the close of the Colonial era. The largest, richest, and most dynamic metropolis of the new world, it even rivaled most urban centers of the old.[2] It was in many ways a remarkable city, but one of its most striking features was its artisan community. Throughout the Revolutionary era, both natives and visitors marveled at the extent and quality of the manufacturing carried on in Philadelphia.[3]

During the Colonial period, the growth of manufacturing activity in Philadelphia was considered by some to be anomalous, and even threatening. General Thomas Gage, one of the most perceptive analysts of America in His Majesty's service, discussed the problem in urgent language:

> During my Stay at Philadelphia, I could not help being surprized at the great Increase of that City in Buildings, Mechanicks and Manufactures. The Emigrations from Great Britain and Ireland and the Importation of Germans every year from Holland,

contribute to the constant Increase of Mechanicks and Manufacturers in this Province beyond any of the rest. The discharged Soldiers too have contributed a little to this Increase in Philadelphia, as well as in other Cities of the Continent. Instead of clearing uncultivated Lands, which it was expected they would do, they have for the most part crowded into the Towns to work at Trades, and help to Supply the Inhabitants with Necessarys, which should be imported from the Mother Country. . . .

They talk and threaten much in other Provinces of their Resolutions to lessen the importation of British Manufactures, and to Manufacture for themselves; but they are by no means able to do it. The People of Pennsylvania lay their plans with more Temper and Judgment, and pursue with Patience and Steadfastness. They don't attempt Impossibilities, or talk of what they will do, but are silently stealing in Mechanicks and Manufacturers; and if they go on as they have hitherto done, they will probably in a few years Supply themselves with Many Necessary Articles, which they now import from Great Britain.[4]

The "constant Increase of Mechanicks and Manufacturers" which General Gage observed was a faulty cog in the British mercantile engine. Imperial theory called for Americans to engage in agriculture and extractive industries, making for themselves only the few simple necessities which could not be manufactured conveniently and economically in England.[5]

Nor were Englishmen the only ones concerned about this phenomenon: during the 1760s and 1770s, Philadelphia merchants often worried about the social, economic, and political presence of mechanics. Something had begun to go wrong in Philadelphia during the third quarter of the eighteenth century. Mechanics, whose economic activity was contrary to imperial ideals, and whose social and political aspirations cut across the grain of prevailing patterns, began to place unfamiliar demands on the structures and processes of the community. This development had a profound impact on the character of the American Revolution in Philadelphia. It gave force and substance to the home-rule movement, and it helped to determine "who should rule at home."[6]

It is impossible to date precisely the beginning of Philadelphia's manufacturing challenge, for in a sense it had existed from the beginning. But by the close of the Seven Years' War it was more pronounced than it ever had been before. Nearly a decade of wartime economic boom had encouraged the growth of American artisan trades far beyond the bounds intended by those who created and maintained the Empire. A postwar depression notwithstanding, the lure of "the mechanical arts" remained high in a growing city which demanded an ever expanding number and variety of goods and services.[7] By 1765, there was hardly a craft known to Western man not practiced in Philadelphia, and many of the practitioners rivaled the skill of the best English and European artisans.

Owen Biddle, an erstwhile clockmaker turned merchant, made a poignant testimony in 1771, when he wrote an English factor,

> Notwithstanding the Clocks thou sent were exceeding Good in Quality, yet such is the small demand for them as well as Watches at this time, that I have no encouragement to order any now, many Workmen having come from Great Britain in that Branch of Business, who execute their work well and afford it as low as they can be imported. This is like to be the case, with most branches of Manufacture which we are now supplied with from your parts in Course of time as we have every advantage for such an undertaking, except hands, which increase amazingly daily.[8]

It was one thing for American manufacturers to challenge the English in the simple crafts—soap-boiling, iron-mongering, and the like—but in Philadelphia the challenge was being successfully mounted in all artisan trades, including clock-making and cabinet-making, two of the most advanced crafts in the British Empire.[9]

Numerically, manufacturing Philadelphians accounted for a larger segment of the city's population than any other social or economic group.[10] It was inevitable that this burgeoning community would cast an important influence on the Revolutionary movement.

PHILADELPHIA ARTISANS

Leather Crafts	Clothing Crafts	Shipbuilding Crafts
cordwainer	tailor	shipwright
shoemaker	hatter	boat-builder
glover	stocking-weaver	sail-maker
saddler	milliner	mast-maker
harness-maker	stay-maker	rope-maker
breeches-maker	dyer & bleacher	ship-rigger
tanner	mantua-maker	block-maker
currier	hairdresser	anchor-maker
skinner	fringe-weaver	ship-carver
	tape and ribbon-weaver	ship-painter

Clock & Jewellery Crafts	Printing & Paper Crafts	Fine Arts Crafts
		miniaturist
jeweller	printer	hair-worker
goldsmith	engraver	artist
silversmith	stationer	
clock-maker	book-binder	Boiling Crafts
watch-maker	paper-maker	
instrument-maker	parchment-maker	candle-maker
		soap-boiler

*A list of the principal artisan trades plied in Philadelphia appears here. Space does not permit the inclusion of the many minor, specialized crafts. It is not within the scope of this work to study the craft activities of the various urban trade groups. This subject has received definitive treatment in Carl Bridenbaugh, *The Colonial Craftsman* (New York: New York University Press, 1950), chs. III and IV.

Food & Tobacco Crafts	Construction Crafts	Furniture Crafts
	house-carpenter	cabinet-maker
mustard-maker	brick-layer	chair-maker
chocolate-maker	brick-maker	upholsterer
snuff maker	painter	wall-paperer
beer brewer	plasterer	fan-maker
butcher	wheelwright	carver
baker	stone-cutter	gilder
tobacconist	glazier	turner
distiller	coach-maker	wire-worker
sugar-refiner	plane-maker	coffin-maker
		whip & cane-maker

Pottery Crafts	Forging Crafts	Comb Crafts
potter	smith	comb-maker
glazer	blacksmith	brush-maker
china-maker	white smith	reed-maker
glass-maker	iron-monger	card-maker
	brass-founder	
Container Crafts	cutler	
	tinsmith	
stave-maker	gunsmith	
cooper	pewterer	
	tin plate-maker	
	nailer	

The Manufacturing Community

Ｉｎ eighteenth-century parlance, the terms "mechanic," "artisan," "craftsman," and "tradesman" had both synonymous and ambiguous definition. Sometimes they were used as reference to the kind of work some men did, and in such instances a "mechanic" would be an individual engaged in "Arts wherein the Hand and Body are more concerned than the Mind," be he servant, slave, journeyman, apprentice, or master craftsman.[1] But the terms also were used as reference to a social class. The mechanic *class* did not include apprentices, servants, and slaves; a society conscious of its social ranks did not confuse categories of men who were wholly without property and the liberties attached to property with another category which enjoyed both economic and civil liberties.[2]

Mechanics were usually among the "middling sort," while apprentices, servants, and slaves were either considered "inferior" in social rank or were members of an artisan's household and therefore without rank in society. Even after the propertyless practitioners of the artisan trades have been ruled out, however, the definition of the mechanic social class is still difficult to render. Were journeymen who worked in the crafts members of the mechanic class? Historians have traditionally assumed they were, and further have assumed that dependent artisan workmen were not only a numerical majority of the class but also carried considerable weight in its activities.[3] We may never have a precise demographic history of Philadelphia showing the relative numbers of apprentices, journeymen, servants, slaves, and master craftsmen, but we know enough about the social structure and social behavior of the urban community to make possible the firm supposition that the mechanic class was preponderantly composed of independent entrepreneurs, not employees, and that in any event the behavior of the class was almost wholly determined by the entrepreneurial element. Far from being common laborers, artisans were usually independent businessmen.[4]

One reason for the large number of master craftsmen in Philadelphia is that it was easy, inexpensive, and legal for any man to hang out his own shingle, no matter what his experience or background in the professed trade.[5] In 1705, the city corporation had enacted an ordinance "for restraining those that are not admitted freemen of this city to keep Open Shops or be master workmen," but this restraint was at first ignored and later forgotten, and it never had the slightest effect on the activities of craftsmen.[6] Moreover, Philadelphia lacked the kind of civic institutions—craft guilds—which put teeth into the medieval regulations of which the 1705 ordinance was a pale reflection.[7] Several Philadelphia guilds were founded in the Colonial period, but none exercised the comprehensive craft control typical of medieval guilds, and only one, the Carpenters Company, survived the Revolution.

At the same time that there were no legal or customary impediments to the assumption of the title "master," there were inducements which encouraged men with craft skills to go into business for themselves. Foremost among these was the unusually high price of labor in American cities. Land was so cheap that it drew men away from the cities and towns, and the small corps of wage-earners who remained naturally commanded a higher price.[8] The effect of this phenomenon was to make journeyman status not more desirable, but less so: most masters who employed hands in their shops preferred apprentices, servants, or (in very few instances) slaves, rather than the high-priced journeymen, thus creating the anomalous situation of a difficult employment market for journeymen, even while wages were kept artificially inflated by a general labor shortage.[9] Many of Philadelphia's master mechanics may have been reluctant entrepreneurs, forced to attempt independent trade undertakings by the unsatisfactory employment situation in the city. Many may have been poorer than some journeymen. But the distinction being made here is based on the type of economic activity in which artisans engaged, not on wealth.[10] What gave cohesion to the mechanic class was the common interests of entrepreneurs.

The industrial organization of eighteenth-century Philadelphia was conducive to entrepreneurship in the artisan trades. Because American artisans received no encouragement from local or imperial governments, urban manufacturing remained a marginal enterprise, small in size, with relatively low capitalization. Imperial regulations had a braking effect on large-scale manufacturing (though Americans were not averse to ignoring legislation like the Iron Act and the Hat Act when it was profitable to do so[11]). The need for power also drove most heavy industry out of the city and into the countryside where the river waters and ready fuel supplies could be harnessed for the operation of forges and mills.[12] During the periods of economic boycott before the war, and during the war itself, several large urban factories were organized and funded by public subscription or lottery, but most of these were temporary establishments, and few survived the war. The general scale of artisan economic activity in the city was sufficiently low that the "new beginner" could expect to enter business with relatively little competitive disadvantage, except in a very few trades requiring expensive equipment.[13]

The small scale of most artisan shops also meant that all the workers—masters as well as servants, apprentices, and journeymen —had to be skilled in every aspect of the craft.[14] Thus hundreds who annually emerged from bond had the skills as well as the motives to enter trade for themselves.[15] As one Philadelphian said, "all the mechanic arts are open to the ingenius."[16] Even artisans who did not manufacture completed finished goods themselves often became masters in their own right rather than wage-earners in someone else's employ. A Philadelphia shop which manufactured fire engines, for example, employed numerous other artisans to provide parts, and in nearly every case these sub-contractors were independent masters, not wage-earners.[17] Shipwrights, too, sub-contracted a great deal of their work to other master craftsmen. At the same time that ship yards employed a good number of journeymen in basic construction, the wrights also brought in specialists—smiths, joiners, sail makers, riggers, painters, and mast-makers, for example—and these men were usually independent entrepreneurs.[18] Throughout the Revolutionary era, scores of master mechanics offered their services, on a sub-contracting basis, to their fellow manufacturers.

The condition of the labor market in Philadelphia not only had the effect of causing masters to prefer servants, slaves, and apprentices over journeymen; it also encouraged the formation of corporate alliances among master artisans in preference to the employment of journeymen by masters. Non-wage-earning hands, while inexpensive, were also relatively unskilled, and the entrepreneur who wished to expand or diversify his trade without taking on journeymen was often under the necessity, therefore, to connect himself with other masters. Sometimes tradesmen made permanent or long-term subcontracting arrangements within their own shops to advance production or to secure the services of a specialist; sometimes they invited in a craftsman with talents in a craft allied to their own in order to help attract a wider market; often they arranged short-term partnerships for the purpose of pooling resources.[19]

The general structure of the manufacturing economy in Philadelphia during the eighteenth century thus leads to the conclusion that the number of master craftsmen working in the city was probably much greater than has been traditionally supposed, and the number of journeymen much smaller. Even if journeymen were more plentiful than this evidence would indicate, it is very clear that the activities of mechanics were governed almost entirely by independent masters. For example, journeymen were excluded from the city's trade guilds.[20] When mechanics organized for political purposes, membership in their committees was restricted to masters, so far as it is possible to tell.[21] The self-employed master craftsmen, it is clear, did not normally take counsel with journeymen or other laborers. Only once during the Revolutionary period is there evidence that journeymen and masters joined hands: in the parade celebrating ratification of the 1787 Constitution, masters, servants, apprentices, and journeymen marched together in craft units. But the chronicler of the event commented, "Rank for a while forgot all its claims," implying that is was uncommon for employees to walk as equals with masters.[22]

Many conditions conspired together to make entrepreneurship easy and normal in Philadelphia's manufacturing community. By the period of the American Revolution, there was undoubtedly an unconscious presumption in most mechanics' minds that the road to success was to be found in independent business ventures. With the absence of barriers, and a good many inducements, most young skilled craftsmen must have considered entrepreneurship a natural way to develop their careers. This psychological orientation was undoubtedly re-enforced by the in-bred quality which the community of artisans developed over the years. While it is true, on the one hand, that the same lack of economic role definition which permitted almost anyone to assume the style "master" also made it possible for artisans to become part-time merchants or shopkeepers, it is also true that most mechanics who developed nonmanufacturing interests—and there were many who did, particularly in the latter part of the Revolutionary era—never lost their primary identity as mechanics. Benjamin Franklin, who moved considerably beyond his original calling, wished his epitaph to record only his artisan trade, which shows the holding power of a mechanic calling. Most mechanics (unlike Franklin) remained mechanics after they adopted new business interests because they spent most of their lives wearing a leather apron. The case of Owen Biddle, for example, was rare: he began his career as an artisan watch-maker, but later became a full-time merchant. He maintained an interest in the trade, insofar as it applied to his astronomical work, and he drew on his knowledge of the craft when he judged the quality of imported watches he sold, but he had no business stake in his original calling, and did not think of himself as a "mechanic."[23]

Although social and economic realities tended to blur class distinctions, and although there were some few individuals whose nonmanufacturing interests were so extensive that they could be considered as only marginally in the mechanic class, nevertheless there was in Philadelphia a large corps of men whose primary business was manufacturing and whose mode of economic activity was entrepreneurial. This group of men formed not only a social class, but a genuine community. It was the maturation of the mechanics as a living community which lay behind the dramatic progress they made as a social class during the Revolutionary period.

The sense of community stemmed, of course, partly from the bare fact of shared experience among tradesmen.[24] There were also more specific ways in which it developed.[25] For example, mechanics were closely woven together by business relationships. Many combinations evolved out of the traditional mode of craft education, the apprenticeship system. It was very common (though by no means universal) for a child to obtain his craft education from his father. Often the son of a craftsman did not follow his father's calling, but when this happened he nearly always apprenticed in another craft, rather than in a non-artisan occupation. When a father searched for a master with whom to entrust his son, he normally looked among his acquaintances, who were usually other tradesmen.

Another common bond within the mechanic community was the business partnership. As in the apprenticeship system, some partnerships were determined by family, and we have already observed how many other craftsmen were allied with one another because of the exigencies of the labor market. In addition, there were scores upon scores of mechanics who for reasons of convenience or coincidence or profit joined hands with their fellows in formal partnerships, sub-contracting agreements, and a host of other business associations. Many, for example, wrought products or engaged in services designed primarily or exclusively for the use of their fellow mechanics. Some Philadelphia tradesmen counted on others to retail their goods when their own shops were disadvantageously located or their reputations were not widespread.

Social as well as economic life in Philadelphia tended to foster a sense of community among mechanics. The tendency of artisans' sons to remain in artisan callings, if not in their fathers' specific trades, helped to bind the community together. The craftsman's daughter, when she married, ordinarily chose an artisan husband, which had the same effect. And when a tradesman died, a fellow artisan often administered his will if he had property to dispose of. The historical records do not tell us much about the day-to-day lives of mechanics, but their frequent appearance together in apprentice-ship arrangements, business connections, marriage records, and estate administrations indicates they were closely knit socially. Moreover, as one of Philadelphia's historians has perceptively ob-served, the density of population in the city led naturally to "street and tavern life."[26] The cramped quarters in modest mechanic dwell-ings, as well as the irregular pace of work or the need to borrow a tool, purchase some supplies, ask some advice, or escape the sum-mer heat, encouraged artisans to frequent one another's shops or public places.

In addition to the many business and social relations between individual tradesmen, the community was also rendered more cohe-sive by the presence of craft organizations. Sometimes these asso-ciations were tied to temporary issues affecting a particular segment of the community, and sometimes they assumed the guise of craft guilds. In either case, organizations were a natural outgrowth of the social structure of the urban community. There was never a single section of town which could be described as the artisans' neighbor-hood (though the largest number of mechanics was crowded into the downtown section in Mulberry Ward), but mechanics in partic-ular crafts did tend to group together. For example, a group of tailors lived contiguously on the south side of Market Street be-tween Front Street and the Delaware River, the intersection of Front and Market Streets was dominated by printing shops, and marine crafts clustered near the docks.[27] These groupings, originally matters of convenience, became the social basis of craft organiza-tions.[28]

One of the earliest records of formal union among mechanics is a declaration of eleven coopers in 1742, disavowing a recent accusation that they had tried to fix the price of oil by covenanting among themselves.[29] In 1763, the city's wheelwrights organized in an attempt to take advantage of a potentially profitable situation which arose out of Philadelphia's street-paving project: the Assem-bly had enacted legislation requiring wagoners, carters, draymen, and porters to use wheels with seven-inch rims in order to protect pavements from damage caused by heavy-laden vehicles with nar-row wheels, and the wheelwrights, hoping to profit from the wagoners' necessity, engaged in non-competitive price-fixing on seven-inch wheels.[30] Their collusion was not altogether successful, but it did demonstrate the ease with which craftsmen could form intra-craft organizations. In 1765, an organization called the White Oaks, probably composed of ship carpenters, participated in the Stamp Act disturbance on the side of the Galloway faction.[31] As the decade moved through the 1760s, such organizations among craftsmen of a single trade became more frequent, and by the 1770s mechanic organizations were formed which embraced cross-sections of the artisan community.

Economic necessity was usually at the root of intra-craft organizations. Philadelphia rope-makers, for example, ran into difficulty in 1766 because they had to rely on a very few merchant-dealers for their supplies of hemp, and these dealers had been selling them a bad product at exorbitant prices. The rope-makers organized and petitioned the Assembly to regulate the merchants who put "short, foul, unmerchantable Hemp into some Part of the Bundles, and covering it over on the Outside with good, long. clean, strong and merchantable Hemp," sold the whole to mechanics at a high price.[32] Merchant-dealers were few and wealthy, and their control of the price and quality of hemp was almost complete. It was profitable for them to export hemp, for it carried an imperial bounty, and so long as the quality product was not made available by interlopers, merchant-dealers could always profitably unload their crudest stock on local rope-makers.[33] Shipwrights faced the same difficulty: lumber prices were driven up by the exportation of local timber on raft ships.[34]

Cordwainers also had to do business with merchant-dealers— leather brokers who "engrossed" or monopolized available supplies of the cordwainers' raw materials. By exporting large quantities and keeping the remainder out of the reach of cordwainers, they were able to drive prices up. Moreover, the engrossers, who sold leather by weight, had it cured and stored in "Cellars and other damp Places," thus assuring heavier loads than when properly dried.[35] The cordwainers' petition was soon joined by the city's saddlers, harness-makers, and others in another petition "respecting the manufacturing monopolizing and exporting of leather."[36] "Hint" expressed the broadest interpretation of the problem: "if Leather is Scarce, Shoes will be dearer, and many People think they are too dear already; so that it is like to become a great and heavy Tax to the Public in general, and the poor in particular unless timely prevented."[37]

The reply to the leather craftsmen was a "Remonstrance from the Tanners of the City of Philadelphia and Counties adjacent."[38] Although this document has the appearance of having been submitted by another mechanic organization, it was undoubtedly the work of leather merchants like Jonathan Meredith, who ran a large tanning yard in connection with his mercantile activities.[39] Leather-tanning was a trade requiring substantial capital, and was most profitably carried on by men who had both considerable means and commercial connections.[40] The laws of supply and demands might have operated effectively had many petty cordwainers been dealing with many small tanners; but the scope of enterprises like Meredith's distorted the city's economy.[41] The cordwainers' only effective weapon against the administration of prices was to organize a political lobby.

Philadelphia's silversmiths, like the rope-makers and cordwainers, found it expedient to organize in the 1760s. They submitted a petition to the Assembly asking for regulations and standards "as to the Fineness of the Silver and Gold to be wrought," hoping to stamp out inferior work.[42] This time the enemy was not powerful merchants controlling raw materials, but inferior workmanship on the part of some craftsmen in the business. Whatever the advantages of the ability to enter an artisan trade without an apprenticeship or "admission" requirement, one of the defects of the freedom was that many practitioners did poor work and their reputations tarnished those of the able craftsmen. The silversmiths and goldsmiths attempted to remedy this problem by organizing themselves and lobbying for legislative regulation of their trade.

Other crafts attempted to regulate practitioners for different reasons and in different ways. Sixty-eight of the city's tailors, for example, founded the Taylors Company of Philadelphia in 1771, hoping to come "under proper Regulations respecting our Buisness [sic]," by which they meant controlling prices and wages of journeymen by the publication of standards.[43] The cordwainers, too, created a guild, the Cordwainers Fire Company. Organized ostensibly as a fire prevention and fighting society, it nevertheless was meant to be a craft guild: it not only used the cordwainers' coat of arms (a medieval guild invention) on its fire buckets, it also gave "Certificates of Character" to members departing the city, and denied membership to candidates who had not served "a regular apprenticeship."[44] Business in the clothing and leather trades was both highly competitive and easy to enter, with the result that quality and prices varied substantially from shop to shop; moreover, the artisans who suffered most were those who produced quality wares, for a customer who could afford high prices often preferred clothes and shoes manufactured in the mother country. It was to remedy this difficult situation that guilds were formed.[45]

The Carpenters Company was the most substantial, and also the only permanent, Philadelphia guild. The Taylors Company failed because, unlike the medieval organizations of which it was a pale copy, membership was voluntary; since the company did not encompass all practicing tailors in the city, it merely institutionalized the already poor competitive position of the tradesmen who made up its ranks.[46] Even when the company's own members defied its price and wage code, it was unable to punish them effectively. John Reedle was twice accused of violating the regulations, once for working "under price" and once for over-paying a journeyman, and Hastings Stackhouse was similarly accused of selling clothes at a low price. Both acquitted themselves by finding loopholes in the regulations, thus defeating the spirit of the system. William Main, accused of over-paying his journeyman, did not even try to defend his practices; he simply left the society.[47]

The Cordwainers Fire Company enjoyed a longer history, perhaps because the orgnization's interest in fire fighting helped hold it together, and perhaps, too, because the members did not attempt price-wage regulations. When the company exercised governing power, as in an attempt to alleviate the difficulties incurred in the "frequent losses Sustained by Sarvents and Apprentices running away," the expenses of the program were met by voluntary subscription.[48] Yet even this inoffensive organization failed to survive the Colonial period. By contrast, the Carpenters Company, founded in the 1720s, was more powerful and prestigious at the end of the era than at the beginning.[49]

During the early 1760s, the Carpenters Company had some temporary difficulties because it attempted the same kind of wage-price controls which later undermined the Taylors Company. The company had always had rules for "measuring and valuing" carpentry, and it had experienced little difficulty enforcing adherence to them, even though only a fraction of the master carpenters in Philadelphia belonged to the guild. A powerful deferential social structure governed the building trades, and a tradesman would ignore at his peril the dictates of the company.[50] Observing that modern architectural innovations necessitated a revision of the standards of assessment, the company printed a new code in 1763; but a number of carpenters broke tradition and refused to accept the revised standards.[51] As in all artisan trades, times were difficult in the early 1760s; competition was becoming increasingly stiff, and at the same time the postwar depression caused many serious economic dislocations. It was not a propitious moment for guild regulations, as many carpenters revealed when they attempted to gain a competitive edge on company members by offering cut-rate services. In 1769, opposition to the company's rules was organized into a rival guild, the Friendship Carpenters Company, which blamed the original group for the "Reproach . . . [that] has lain upon the Profession in a general manner for some time past Owing as they Apprehend to the Different Methods Used in Measuring and Valueing the work which belongs to it."[52] Attempts were made to unite the guild organizations in carpentry, but none succeeded.[53] It was not until 1786 that the city's carpenters resolved their differences and united once again into a single organization.

As a general rule, Philadelphia's craft organizations—including both temporary and permanent and both formal and informal—were failures. The wheelwrights' association crumbled when a few craftsmen undercut the covenanters' price agreement.[54] The rope-makers' and cordwainers' and silversmiths' combinations dissolved when the provincial Assembly turned a deaf ear to their petitions: the rope-makers and cordwainers failed because their requests cut against the grain of the dominant merchants' interests, and the silversmiths' request fell victim to the Assembly's quarrels with the proprietary governor.[55] The Cordwainers Fire Company held its last meeting in 1773, at about the same time the cordwainers' Assembly petitions failed, and the Taylors Company dissolved in 1776, though its economic program had failed some time before.[56] Insofar as these craft organizations were created to control the local market, their demise was probably inevitable. Trade guilds were able to eliminate competition in medieval European towns because the artisan callings were more clearly definable, because the law required artisans to belong to guilds which excluded any but trained and tested masters, and because the markets for manufactured artifacts were fairly stable.[57] None of these conditions pertaining in eighteenth-century Philadelphia.[58] Except in the building trades, mechanics' prices were governed not only by their own costs but by a market dominated by imported wares. This factor, coupled with the high price of American labor, made economic life for most mechanics fiercely competitive; craftsmen in the building trades did not have to deal with imported artifacts on their market (though there was substantial internal competition among carpenters, as the rivalry between the two companies demonstrates), which may explain the eventual survival of their company. All other trade guilds which attempted to control competition were inappropriate to the conditions of the marketplace. Moreover, in all the trades, the lack of a statutory definition of "master" and the guilds' lack of legal standing permitted competition to thrive.

Formal craft organizations did not shape social and economic life in the city the way medieval guilds had, but they did reflect the development of social cohesion within the mechanic class. Notwithstanding artisans' superfluity in the British Empire, and notwithstanding their lack of power and standing in the local social, economic, and political structures, they possessed the potential for emerging as a major force in the community.

The Marketplace

THE marketplace in Philadelphia during the decade before Independence was filled with both frustrations and paradoxes for mechanics. For the most part the economy was depressed in these years, which only intensified the difficult competitive position in which most artisans found themselves.[1] The appearance of trade guilds—a kind of irrational, angry attempt to turn back an ineluctable tide—is indicative of the depth of frustration which penetrated the community. And yet, at the same time, there was a bright side to the picture: many artisans devised imaginative and daring schemes to overcome their competitive disadvantages, and the very imperial policies which impeded general economic growth had the accidental effect of encouraging local manufacturing when a buy-American campaign was launched to conserve specie.[2]

The attempts to secure competitive breathing room by obtaining legislative regulations failed for two reasons. First, artisan petitions moved against the grain of the mercantilist system; for the Assembly to have supported American manufactures would have been tantamount to economic treason. As one unhappy correspondent of the *Pennsylvania Gazette* explained in 1771:

It is sincerely to be lamented, that the mechanic Arts and Manufactures cannot be encouraged by our legislature with the same

19

Propriety that they promote the liberal Arts and Sciences; but it happens some how, that our Mother Country apprehends she has a right to manufacture every Article we consume, except Bread and Meat; . . . in these Circumstances it cannot be doubted, that she would take a great and insuperable Offence to any Colony Legislature that should attempt to encourage domestic Manufactures; . . . were it not for this Impediment, we might expect to see the mechanic Arts soon arrive at great Perfection in this Province.[3]

Beyond this, however, regulation was not in the immediate interests of the colonial legislature, which represented mainly agrarian and merchant constituencies. This can be seen most clearly in the ropemakers' petition, which requested legislation to obstruct a profitable trade supported by imperial bounty.

The slackness of Philadelphia's economy in the 1760s provided a backdrop for the stage on which merchants and mechanics competed. The postwar depression was aggravated and perpetuated by the Currency Act and the Sugar Act.[4] The former gradually eliminated provincial paper money, the principal medium of exchange, while the latter cut off the main source of specie. These economic forces, together with periodic natural fluctuations of the rudimentary capitalist economy, conspired to make business life difficult for Philadelphia's commercial community and especially for the lower and middle segments of it whose margin of solvency was always narrow.[5]

Despite their difficulties, however, mechanics engaged their merchant rivals in lively and often cut-throat contests. The spirit of the marketplace is illustrated by a bitter quarrel begun by one of Philadelphia's cutlers, Stephen Paschall, who claimed that "some merchants of this city have, for these 5 or 6 years past, imported large quantities of sickles, stamped *S. Pachall,* in imitation (as I apprehend) of my stamp, which is *S. Paschall,* and on the credit there of, have sold great quantities . . . and . . . the workmanship is by no means equal."[6] Daniel Offley, Philadelphia's chief resident anchor-maker, opened a similar controversy when he pointed out the poor quality of some anchors being manufactured in New York by William Hauxhurst and sold locally. He accused the merchants who distributed the Hauxhurst anchors of stealing his designs and journeymen; he publicly refused to repair any of the imported anchors and guaranteed his own; and he announced that he would stop making anchors, depriving the city of a quality ware, if Philadelphians persisted in buying the cheaper product.[7] The Colonial mechanics did not often enjoy marketing advantages over merchant rivals, but when they did their protective instincts were fierce and unrelenting. Richard Wistar, a part-time potter, was approached by a merchant for information about the clay used in local potteries, but when he discovered that the information was to be passed on to a potentially competitive pottery in Boston he refused to discuss the matter because he was "apprehensive it may hurt his Business and thinks it not a reasonable request."[8]

The marketing battles which arose between merchants and mechanics were reinforced by fundamental differences in the size and nature of their business enterprises.[9] By contrast with most artisan shops, merchant businesses were large and complex: systems of credit and exchange allowed many to create enormous financial empires, and indeed the nature of the mercantile economy often necessitated large-volume transactions.[10] The lopsided balance of competitive forces caused mechanics continuing difficulties. One Philadelphian drew attention to a typical problem in 1770 when he complained about collusion among local shopkeepers and merchants to drive out public vendues, or auctions, by agreement to boycott any in which unit prices were less than £5 and any in which the auctioneer was known to be selling privately to parties other than merchants or shopkeepers. "A Mechanic" predicted that should the agreement succeed, "the great shopkeepers will swallow up the little ones so that one half of our small dealers, who depend solely on buying their goods at vendue, must decline that business, as they cannot find money sufficient to supply themselves in a large way."[11]

Mechanics liked to shop for bargains and often were able to work profitably by purchasing raw materials in odd-sized lots, but the shopkeepers' covenant would have made this impossible. The motives behind this tradesman's complaint differed little from those of the rope-makers and cordwainers who tried to stop the monopolizing activities of their principal suppliers. There were "many discontented spirits" among cordwainers when the Assembly responded to their petition by passing a law which regulated the cordwainers (imposing restrictions which would make their wares more expensive in a market where they were already hard pressed by the competition of imported English shoes), but which was shot through with loopholes from the merchant-dealers' standpoint.[12] Specifically, although the statute appeared to limit the possibility of merchant-dealers gaining direct control of the cordwainers' leather supply by prohibiting the sale of engrossed leather in the city (except in the market, where open, competitive bidding usually drove the price down anyway), the act of engrossing itself was not proscribed, nor was there anything to prevent engrossers from keeping the supply short (and the price high) by exporting large quantities.[13]

Unequal though the balance of economic and political power between merchant and mechanic was, however, it does not appear to have daunted Philadelphia's manufacturers. The first line of battle was taken in the advertising columns of the city's newspapers. To defend the segment of the market which they were gradually winning for their wares, artisans made claims of superior craftsmanship; they lauded the special virtues of Philadelphia-made artifacts; and they tried to make their own work more attractive by offering services not afforded customers who bought foreign goods. Overcoming Philadelphians' prejudices against native tradesmen required a considerable public relations campaign. Joseph Stiles, fishing tackle maker, for example, advertised that his equipment was "as neatly fitted as at any Fishing Tackle Shop in London"; William Calverley, weaver, claimed his white cotton counterpanes were "flowered as neat, and better than any imported"; William Richards, cork-cutter, announced that his corks would be sold "much cheaper than can be imported"; Abraham Shelly, thread-maker and tape-weaver, claimed his work was "superior to any imported from Europe, for strength, evenness, fineness and cheapness"; William Ross, cordwainer, got the best of both worlds by announcing that he had imported leather and worsted from England "for the greater Satisfaction of his customers," and also that his finished product was "Equal in Goodness to any made in England."[14]

Many Philadelphia mechanics realized that they must offer

more than a claim to equal "goodness" or "cheapness" with English imports if they were to attract customers. John Wood, a clock and watch-maker, for example, advised Pennsylvanians to buy "Philadephia-made" watches, because they could always depend upon the makers, who had reputations to protect, to make good in the event of a breakdown.[15] Other craftsmen offered special services to their customers in order to stimulate sales. John Fromberger, furrier, advertised free fur storage to those who bought his furs in preference to imported; Nathanael Cope, smith, offered to clean the smoke and roasting jacks he made for local customers; Moses Judah, embroiderer, announced that he would visit customers' homes if they were unable to get to his shop; John Marie, tailor, offered to dry clean clothes "in the best manner, without the unnecessary trouble of ripping or washing."[16] It was common for a tradesman to advertise that he performed his craft "in all its branches," which was a more general way of offering something more to Philadelphians who chose to patronize American manufacturers.

Other mechanics tried different strategies to get the edge on their competitors. The location of one's business, then as now, often made a difference. One useful tactic was to move into the shop vacated by a mechanic of reputation. This is doubtless what prompted John Wood, a famous clock-maker, to advertise that "Mr. Henry Snelling, who now carries on business [at Wood's former] place is not nor has been any way connected with the said Wood."[17] In a few trades business could be stimulated by making it known that one was well acquainted with the styles and methods of European and English craftsmen.[18] And some artisans found that they were most successful when specializing in a particular aspect of a craft.[19] Others who had substantial resources began to carry the raw materials of their trade which they not only used themselves but also sold to fellow craftsmen.[20]

Many mechanics in Philadelphia discovered that the key to effective marketing was comprehensiveness.[21] It was undoubtedly with this in mind that many began carrying imported wares in their shops. They could stock certain foreign goods which were in high demand to attract customers, and supplement their inventories with their own fabrications. Moreover, if their own goods were, in fact, cheaper or better than imported, the comparison would be plain for the customer to see. Thus, for example, John Wood, the clock-maker who publicly advised Philadelphians to buy the work of local artisans because they could be depended upon to stand behind their workmanship, carried a large assortment of imported watches and clocks.[22] Goldsmiths, silversmiths, and jewellers nearly always carried imported merchandise. Some, like Joseph Richardson, used European artifacts as a source of design, while others used them merely to supplement their own works.[23] Printers and bookbinders engaged heavily in the import business, as did the hatters.[24] Three Philadelphia smiths sold imported goods, such as "a large assortment of best London pewter."[25] By the 1780s, eight tailors had become so involved in the sale of imported clothing that they listed themselves as "merchant-tailor" in the city directory.[26]

The heavy competition also moved some mechanics to seek markets for their goods outside the city by selling to "Country Store keepers, Shallop-men, Waggoners, and others."[27] It was common for artisans to give "large allowances to those who buy to sell again."[28] One rope-maker took his manufactures "in the Country to Traffick for Hemp and Flax, etc.," thereby both dealing with the problem of securing raw materials and selling his finished product.[29] While some were content to "traffick" in the hinterland, other more ambitious craftsmen exported their products to other Continental and Caribbean ports. Exporting was not possible for most, but in some well-developed trades such as furniture-making, Philadelphia's reputation assured the tradesman of a market anywhere in British America.[30] Two of the city's cutlery shops, Wylie and Goucher, and Samuel Wheeler, manufactured "any kind of Iron Work for the West-Indies, or elsewhere"; the wire-working partnership of Nathan and David Sellers exported its work to New York; Joseph Cooke and Company, jewellers and silversmiths, sold some of their wares in the southern colonies; Daniel Offley not only drove imported anchors off the local market, he also managed to export some of his own; Timothy Matlack, beer brewer (and future radical politician), offered to supply masters of vessels with his "Philadelphia brewed bottled beer, remarkably pale, and very good."[31] Printers had a very special kind of export business—the trade in ideas—which extended to every major population center in North America. William God-dard's *Chronicle,* which had the widest circulation in the colonies, listed seventy-four outlets.[32] Exportation by Philadelphia's manu-facturers was not a massive business, but it was an element of sig-nificance for many artisans.[33]

Not all mechanics were successful, however, in securing a market for their wares, either at home or abroad. Philadelphia pot-ters, for example, faced what they regarded as insuperable difficul-ties. They could not sell cheap, utilitarian redware and earthenware in the hinterland, for the countryside abounded with small potteries which supplied local needs, and it was impossible to produce white-ware and porcelain for the discriminating Philadelphia market which had access to English china. The only substantial attempt to obtain a part of the market for local china was made by Gousse Bonnin and George Anthony Morris, Jr., who set up a china and porcelain works in the Southwark district of the city in 1769. Their product was crude, however, by comparison with the work of En-glish manufactories, and did not satisfy the refined tastes of the city's principal buyers.[34] An appeal to the Assembly for financial aid (based on the premise that during the non-importation crisis their undertaking deserved public support) netted them nothing, and when large amounts of English china flooded the market after the partial repeal of the Townshend Duties, the works had to be closed.[35] The potters' experience is an emphatic example of the problem ulti-mately faced by all American tradesmen. An ingenious mechanic, one with unusual gifts or large personal resources, might succeed, but they were the few. Most mechanics lived dangerously close to bankruptcy a good part of the time. Under these circumstances, it was almost inevitable that members of the aggressive manufacturing community in Philadelphia would begin to consider ways in which they might reorient the local market and their fellow citizens' atti-tude toward home manufactures. It was not enough that mechanics' wares were of good quality and relatively inexpensive: if they were to obtain a permanent hold it would be necessary to invent ways to create presumptions in their favor.

The economic and political repercussions of Great Britain's at-tempts to reorganize the Empire after the Seven Years' War provided ideal opportunities for Philadelphia tradesmen. The Sugar Act and the Currency Act of 1764 were a mixed blessing. Insofar as they tended to depress Philadelphia's commercial economy by draining specie and liquidating paper medium, manufacturers suffered as much as merchants, and sometimes more.[36] Yet this economic situation held a hidden benefit, too: the evaporation of money would continue under the new imperial legislation only to the degree that Americans bought goods from England, and this was a powerful argument for buying home manufactures, as artisans pointed out repeatedly.[37] Richard Wistar, brass-button-maker, lectured his fellow Philadelphians: "as the Scarcity of money renders it difficult to make Remittances for Merchandise had from Great-Britain, it is hoped that a proper Encouragement will be given to the Manufactures of our own country."[38] Benjamin Jackson, ink-powder-maker, put it less stridently, but just as plainly: "N.B. As all our home manufactures are attended with obvious good consequences to the city and province, and help to keep and circulate money among us . . . it is hoped this (tho' little manufactory) will meet with encouragement."[39]

Throughout the decade of the 1760s, Philadephians struggled to manage their economy in order to conserve specie at home, and the claims being made by these and scores of other mechanics fitted nicely into the scheme. John Dickinson had stated the case well when he wrote: "We have our choice of two things—to continue our present limited and disadvantageous commerce—or to promote manufactures among ourselves, with a habit of economy, and thereby remove the necessity we are now under of being supplied by Great-Britain."[40] This concept permitted mechanics to combine patriotism with profit, and it was not the last time they would utilize the argument.

With the stage having been set by the depression of the Philadelphia economy, the reaction to the Stamp Act was almost predictable. When Thomas Wharton complained to Benjamin Franklin that the Stamp Act would drain the Colonies' fiscal resources "which will oblige Us, at last to manufacture among ourselves," he was voicing a common opinion.[41] Later in the year, mechanics not only had a strong argument favoring local manufactures, they also had the reality of a protected market when the Non-Importation Resolutions were adopted. The Resolutions stopped up the trade which brought to market foreign wares, and they urged Philadelphians "to be frugal in their use and consumption of all Manufactures excepting those of *America*."[42] Besides the market protection afforded by the agreement, commercial disruption would mean a decline in the exportation of foodstuffs and raw materials, causing agricultural over-production; the consequent drop in the value of land would drive country yeomen into the city to find employment manufacturing "many Articles which [they] would otherwise be enabled, and would chuse, to take from England."[43] Should the protest be extended over a long period of time, the labor shortage—the factor which drove up the price of American wares—would be mitigated and the competitive position of mechanics enhanced.

The Stamp Act crisis ended in 1766, but not before it had established a new set of ideas in the minds of all Philadelphians, and especially of the tradesmen. Insofar as the novelties of the postwar British Empire tended to impoverish America, her salvation was to become in some measure self-sufficient—to find the means for doing without the foreign trade which was being used to rob the Colonists of their fortunes and their liberties. In short, Philadelphians began to re-think their attitudes toward the local market, to value more highly the capacities of struggling mechanics. What emerged was nothing short of embryonic economic nationalism, predating Independence by a decade.[44] It emerged with the substantial help of mechanics, who took every occasion to equate patronage of home manufactures with patriotism. Alexander Rutherford advertised that he wished "to inform such of the ladies of Philadelphia, as are resolved to distinguish themselves by their patriotism and encouragement of American manufactures, that he makes and sells all sorts of worsted shoes, of all sizes, as neat and cheap as any imported from England."[45] Daniel Mause, in a similar vein, advertised that he had "erected looms for manufacturing thread and cotton stockings, hoping the good People of this and the neighboring Provinces will encourage this his Undertaking at a time when *America* calls for the Endeavours of her *Sons*."[46]

Some Philadelphians were able to shrug off the question of the self-sufficiency of the local economy after the repeal of the Stamp Act, but others were not. While a group of gentlemen expressed their satisfaction by giving their homespun (the symbol of the movement to do without foreign manufactures) to the poor, the mechanics undoubtedly observed the end of non-importation with reluctance.[47] For the first time in the history of America, public policy had been shifted in favor of home manufactures, and the artisans cannot have been happy when the trade barriers were let down. At any rate, when a second major imperial crisis arose in 1768, the mechanics did not hesitate immediately to recast their arguments in the mold forged in 1765. As early as January of 1768, "Oeconomicus" was recommending "a disuse of all foreign superfluities" and the patronage of local artisans.[48] Later that year, Richard Mason, the fire-engine-maker, solicited the business of local fire companies, commenting that "the times call upon us to unite in promoting by every means in our power, the establishing [of] manufactures, &c. among ourselves."[49] A year later, the Friendship, Hibernian, Union, Britannia, and Sun fire companies responded by chipping in to purchase a Mason engine for the House of Employment, for which Mason thanked them, saying they had generously encouraged "a Fellow-Citizen in a Branch of Business, which, it is hoped, may be carried on to the Satisfaction of his future Employers, as well as save them the Trouble and Risque of importing so necessary an Article from foreign Parts."[50] Even the conservative city Corporation may have been moved by a patriotic spirit when it employed the local engine-maker in 1769.[51]

Robert and Thomas Kennedy, map-makers, were content to advertise themselves as "lovers of art and their Country."[52] Philadelphia's glass-makers had one of the most obvious arguments in favor of their trade, since one of the Revenue Acts taxed English glass. Four of them collectively purchased advertising space in the local papers to announce that they would buy broken glass which they intended to "work up" again in a new glass factory shortly to be opened. "It is hoped all Lovers of American Manufacture, will encourage what lies in their Power," they said, "and particularly in this Instance, save, collect, and send such broken Glass" to the subscribers. Their parting caveat: "N.B. No Duties Here!"[53] Once again, mechanics' advertising associated their business activity with patriotism, as William Evans, tailor, who identified himself with "all lovers of liberty and generous dealing."[54]

The non-importation agreement adopted by Philadelphia's commercial community in 1768 spoke to the general economic problems of America, as well as to the more specific issue of the Revenue Acts, and it once more identified home manufacturing as the key to the Colonies' salvation: "if those Acts of Parliament which prohibit us from a Circuitous Trade, restain us from a proper Medium of Commerce, impose Duties on British Manufactures, and oppress us with other Burthens and Difficulties . . . are continued, the People of America, must from Necessity, if not from Motives of Interest, set up Manufactures of their own."[55] "A Tradesman" later recalled that mechanics supported the agreement unanimously, because those who suffered were "but few, when compared to the Number of those who have received great Benefit from it."[56]

The efforts to develop home manufactures were more substantial during the period 1768–70 than they had been during the Stamp Act crisis, and they involved many Philadelphians other than the artisans.[57] When "Colonus" said in 1769, "it is unquestionably our highest interest to manufacture for ourselves so far as we have materials," he voiced a general public sentiment, not a peculiarly mechanic opinion.[58] Samuel Coates, a prominent merchant, wrote to an English acquaintance: "We Shall by Repeated Oppression be Stimulated to Encrease and Establish Manufactures, which will in a little Time Rise to great Perfection. We have made great Progress in Some branches Already, in particular in the Manufacture of Snuf and Hosiery of all kinds, and Cutlery of many sorts."[59]

The snuff manufacture which Coates mentioned was undertaken by Miers Fisher, one of the wealthiest merchants of the city, in parnership with Thomas Gilpin, also a merchant.[60] Alexander Bartram took time off from his counting house to enter a pottery business in 1767, and was soon claiming that his wares were "allowed by the nicest Judges to exceed any imported from England."[61] These and other merchants who adopted manufacturing interests quickly learned about the competitive problems of the American artisan.

Although a number of merchants took up manufacturing ventures as individuals, the corporate manufactory, in which the adventurers had only a financial interest, was more common. The most famous such project was undertaken by members of the American Philosophical Society, called the Society for the Cultivation of Silk.[62] It was preceded and succeeded by numerous other ventures. The Philosophical Society also attempted to aid paper manufacturing in 1773 by beginning a campaign to collect old linen rags.[63] As early as 1766, the discontinuance of drawbacks on foreign linen had resulted in the formation of a company to employ Philadelphia's poor in the manufacture of linen.[64] In 1772, a special lottery was run for the encouragement of an American Steel Manufactory, and throughout the period from 1768 until Independence there were numerous attempts to establish the manufacture of woolens.[65] The degree of merchant participation in these various projects reflects a changing attitude within the mercantile community. Perhaps Charles Thomson was not atypical when he jotted down the following "General Maxims of Trade":

> A Trade may be of benefit to the Merchants and injurious to the body of the nation & v.v.
> The Exportation of manufactures is in the highest degree beneficial to a nation.
> The Exportation of Superfluities is so much clear gain.
> The Importation of foreign materials to be manufactured by us, instead of importing manufactured Goods, is saving a great deal of Money.
> The Exchanging Commodities for Commoditys is generally an Advantage.
> All Imports of Goods which are reexported have a real benefit.
> The letting Ships to freight to other Nations is profitable.
> The Imports of things absolutely necessary, cannot be esteemed bad.
> The importing Commoditys of mere Luxury is so much real loss as they amount to.
> The Importation of such goods as hinder the Consumption of our own or check the progress of any of our manufactures is a visible disadvantage & irreparibly tends to ruin of multitudes.

*   *   *   *

The best way to preserve Commerce is to recommend the Preservation of the best markets for the Products & Manufactures of our native Country.

The first & best market of any Country are the natives & Inhabitants of that Country.[66]

It is less important that the new manufacturing enterprises were seldom successful than that they influenced the attitudes of Philadelphians. As Thomas Clifford put it: " 'tis a truth may be depended on that we are constantly improving in things necessaty puts us upon attempting; matters of that sort once gone into will I believe not be hastily laid aside."[67] Benjamin Rush expressed the same idea:

The grand complaint with laborers among us is that we do not pay them sufficient prices for their work. A plain reason may be assigned for this; we consume too little of their manufactures to keep them employed the whole year round; their wages therefore must of consequence be proportionately higher during the few months they do work; but as soon as American manufactures become general, this complaint will have no foundation, and hundreds of artificers of every kind would be invited to come over from England and settle among us.[68]

The crisis which precipitated the first non-importation agreement had resolved itself in 1766, and although it is fairly clear that mechanics' commitment to a reoriented market carried beyond the crisis period, they had no reasonable argument for perpetuating non-importation or other policies favoring home manufactures after repeal of the odious act. This was not the case in 1770, however, and as a result the arguments set forth by mechanics and some merchants during the immediate crisis were sustained during the months and years after merchants rescinded their non-importation resolution.[69] "A Citizen" argued that a few dry-goods merchants had defaulted as the protectors of American liberties, and demanded: "Let the Powers of Patriotism be drawn from their *proper Source*. Let the landholders, Artificers and independent freemen of this province take upon themselves the defense of those liberties in which they have the greatest and most substantial interest."[70] A year later a correspondent of the *Pennsylvania Chronicle* sardonically declared he was "amazed that the judicious Advocates for Liberty should omit to give us their sage Opinion on the fatal Consequences that must result from our large Importation from Great-Britain, and our almost total Neglect of our own Manufactures, the most durable Source of Wealth and Independence."[71] And mechanics in all trades continued to harp on the matter in their newspaper advertisements.[72]

As the imperial crisis deepened, there can be no question that the American response to oppression directly affected Philadelphia's manufacturing community and was, in turn, influenced by the mechanics. At the same time that they experienced hard times when the commercial economy was disrupted, artisans also began to benefit from the new attitudes being adopted toward the local market by their fellow Americans. Moreover, there can be no question that mechanics, realizing the benefits they were reaping, were beginning to enter actively into the political structure which emerged to cope with the crisis.

The Emergence of the Mechanics
in Politics, 1765–70

T HE communities of mechanics in eighteenth-century American cities have fascinated historians since they were first brought to the forefront by scholars writing in the Progressive Era. The Progressive historians assumed mechanics were an excluded class—excluded from politics by high franchise requirements, excluded from economic opportunities by the preeminence and power of merchants, excluded from upward social mobility by insurmountable class barriers—and that during the Revolution they strove, as a class, against the structures and institutions which had deprived them.[1] These historians correctly sensed changing moods and attitudes among urban common men, beginning in the decade before Independence; yet this phenomenon was based neither on a class-conscious feeling of exclusion nor on a perception of traditional social, economic, and political institutions as without potential to work in their interests. On the contrary, the striking feature of the decade from 1765 until 1775 was the recognition within the artisan community that although existing institutions were not at that time favorably disposed toward the mechanics, the fault lay in the uses to which institutions were put, not in the institutions themselves.[2]

Radicalism in Philadelphia during the pre-Independence decade, in other words, consisted not in harsh class-conscious or Jacobin attitudes; rather, it was characterized by the desires of a burgeoning community of manufacturing entrepreneurs with continuing and accelerating upward social, economic, and political aspirations to reorient existing structures and patterns of behavior. Artisans' disappointment and frustration with the failures of the political system to recognize and support their legitimate economic concerns, for example, resulted not in abandonment of the economic system or the political structure which supported it, but in persevering efforts to affect changed consumer attitudes in Philadelphia and to encourage governmental support. Sometimes mechanics' efforts resulted in their participation in extra-legal political groups, yet even here the objective was not to overturn the system so much as to make it operate more efficiently and effectively and responsively in a crisis with which it was not designed to cope.

An examination of Philadelphia's social institutions—the foundations of all Philadelphians' lives—reveals that artisans were neither arbitrarily excluded nor, for the most part, so estranged as to contemplate radical reconstruction of the city's social milieu. It is true that a very few of Philadelphia's social clubs, such as the Mount Regale Fishing Company and the Jockey Club, were exclusive in their membership, but there is no evidence that mechanics ever contemplated crashing their barriers.[3] Most clubs and societies in which it is reasonable to suppose mechanics might have had an interest did not restrict them from membership. All the fire companies, for example, were socially integrated except one, which excluded everyone *except* tradesmen (the Cordwainers Fire Company).[4] Philadelphia also had a number of social clubs for peoples of particular national backgrounds, whose stated purpose was charitable (but whose real activities were much broader), and these societies, as well, usually blurred class distinctions.[5] The St. Andrews Society and the Society of the Sons of St. George, organizations of Scotsmen and Englishmen, included both merchants and artisans in their membership lists.[6] Sometimes these organizations expressed views favorable toward mechanics, as when the Sons of St. George declared that "As the Society do not proceed upon narrow Principles, but will assist their poor Countrymen in a Way which will be also Advantageous to the Community, Artificers and

Manufacturers coming into this Province, and being Natives of England, or Sons of Englishmen, shall be encouraged and assisted by the Society more abundantly than those who are not of any Trade or Calling."[7]

Not only is it clear that many social and civic clubs like fire companies and nationality associations tended not to segregate the two large entrepreneurial classes in Philadelphia; there is also evidence that the limited separation of classes which did pertain in some areas was breaking down in the 1760s. There was a general movement in the city toward the union of societies in similar fields. The most famous, of course, was the conjunction of the two principal philosophical societies.[8] The literary community also began to consolidate when in 1766 the Amicable Library Company, a small organization which never published a catalog or a list of its members, was absorbed by the Union Library Company. In 1768, the Union Company was again augmented by the absorption of the Association Library Company, a society begun by craftsmen, aping the Library Company of Philadelphia, which had had the effect of segregating artisans, at least in their literary pursuits. And in 1769, the amalgamation process was completed by the uniting of the city's two major subscription libraries, the Union Library Company and the Library Company of Philadelphia.[9] On the eve of the Revolution, the Library Company was not only a large organization, it also included men from all walks of life.

Notwithstanding its lack of medieval caste, Philadelphia society was not exactly egalitarian. In the social, as in the economic sphere, mechanics were working against patterns which largely ignored, even if they did not exclude, men of their station. The point is, however, that arbitrary and absolute exclusion—the root of class-conscious radicalism—was absent in Philadelphia. The same generalizations can be made about the political history of the city. For although Philadelphia always was rent with discord, parties and factions were not based primarily on class considerations.[10] As the Revolutionary era elapsed, artisans' ideas and attitudes became more clearly defined, and as a community they were often at odds with prevailing political groups; yet they never became isolated at the radical end of the political spectrum, nor did they dominate extra-legal politics. Radicalism in the city encompassed a wide range of social ranks, from the wealthiest gentlemen to the poorest laborers.

The story of Pennsylvania's politics during the 1760s contains one of the great ironies of Colonial American political history. It was a period of democratic growth which effectively impeded the colony's participation in America's great democratic revolution. Viewed outside the context of the imperial crisis which began in 1764, what was happening has the appearance of a classic case of emergent American democracy: an indigenous, elected political body, the provincial Assembly, contested every prerogative, every power, and every privilege held by the alien proprietary governor. The jealous and tenacious Quaker Party, led by Benjamin Franklin and Joseph Galloway, condemned Penn family tax evasion, denounced the inflexible and secret instructions given by the Proprietor to his governors, and ultimately attempted to convince George III to void the proprietary contract and place the colony under royal auspices.[11]

One unfortunate and *un*democratic result of the fixed attention the Assembly gave to its battle against the Proprietor was that many legitimate needs of its constituencies were sacrificed. A minor illustration is contained in the story of the goldsmiths and silversmiths, who became victims of a contest over the governor's prerogative to take part in the appointment of civil officers: the proposed legislation to set standards "as to the Fineness of Silver and Gold to be wrought" attempted to deny the governor a legitimate prerogative by excluding him from participation in the choice of an assay officer; since the governor refused to approve the bill while it contained provisions that would erode his power, and since the Assembly refused to amend it to meet his single objection, the artisans' plea for regulation withered on the vine.[12] Another, far more egregious result of the Assembly's fixation was that its members missed the significance of the imperial innovations introduced between 1764 and 1768, and were unable to adjust their thinking to fit new realities, with the result that Pennsylvania was prevented from playing a leadership role in the early phases of the Revolution. At precisely the time when close association with, and dependence upon, the

British Crown was coming into question, Pennsylvania's Assembly, under the aegis of the Quaker Party, was in the midst of a pitched battle to destroy the old constitution and cast the colony on the mercies of the King and his ministers.[13]

Neither the Quaker Party, which dominated the provincial Assembly, nor the Proprietary faction, which represented the Penn family's interests, represented Philadelphia's mechanics during the 1760s. The explanation for this is not that artisans were disfranchised or otherwise politically excluded, but that the forces operating in provincial politics were simply irrelevant to the artisan community. As one careful historian has observed, Pennsylvania politics consisted in "essentially a private quarrel between rival [Proprietary and Quaker] gentleman leaders, and scarcely affected the people at all."[14] Recent scholarship has shown that the Proprietary faction, long believed to have drawn together "disfranchised mechanics" and "under represented frontiersmen," did nothing of the kind (the two were, in fact, hostile); the Proprietary faction was no more representative of Philadelphia mechanics' interests than the Quaker.[15]

It is necessary to reject the notion of Progressive historians that mechanics were part of a lower-class political movement which coalesced in the Proprietary faction in the mid-1760s, where it developed a political foundation which carried it through the Revolutionary era. The evidence for such a conclusion simply does not exist.[16] Neither is it proper, however, to accept the conclusions of some recent scholars who picture mechanics as part of the conservative Quaker establishment in the 1760s. It has been argued that the dominant Quaker Party was engaged in the "politics of ingratiation"—an increasingly vain and misguided attempt to win favor for the Assembly's Privy Council petition (to transform Pennsylvania from a Proprietary to a Royal colony) by cooperating with the imperial government, including its attempts to introduce novel taxation measures in 1765 and 1768—and that mechanics joined forces with the ingratiators.[17] It is true that Pennsylvania's reaction to the Stamp Tax was mild, also that the superbly organized Quaker Party acted vigorously to bring about this result (the Proprietary faction, even though it recognized the political capital inherent in the Quaker position was unable to organize for effective political participation in 1765).[18] As William Bradford explained: "our Body [of Sons of Liberty] in this city is not declared numerous, as unfortunate dissentions in Provincial politics keep us a rather divided people."[19] The evidence that the artisan community actively backed the Quaker Party is, however, very thin.

There is documentary proof of only one mechanic group supporting the Galloway-Franklin faction. This was an organization of ship carpenters known as the White Oaks.[20] Galloway once wrote that in 1765, everything proposed by the radicals "was hissed or opposed by Some of the W Oaks . . . who were there," and Samuel Wharton reported to Franklin that the Quaker election ticket of 1765 had been supported by "every Mechanick, who rowed you from Chester to the Ship"—that is, the White Oaks—who had "associated for the Preservation of Peace in the city."[21] Other than this group of artisans, we know of none which *actively* participated in the Quaker Party's machinations. But why, we may ask, did other mechanics apparently passively acquiesce, allowing the Quaker program to succeed? Why did not the city's tradesmen become embroiled in violent turmoil such as occurred in New York, as Philadelphia's own radical leaders hoped and expected they would?[22]

The best explanation lies in the fact that violence was avoided because merchants were in the process of adopting a measure which promised to protest the Stamp Act effectively—more effectively than violent demonstration—at the same time that it would coincidentally promote home manufactures. Again, it must be emphasized that mechanics were not shiftless dependent laborers, liable to act irresponsibly and capable of easy manipulation by either radical incendiaries or Quaker grandees. They were mainly independent entrepreneurs who had a clear grasp of their economic situation *vis-a-vis* the other principal economic group, the merchants. They recognized the importance of non-importation for their interests as home manufacturers. They must surely also have recognized the inappropriateness of lawlessness and violence for their interests as businessmen, and it was undoubtedly for this reason that they and other "men of charcter," rather than the rabble, dominated the extra-legal politics of 1765.[23]

The political maneuvering of the Galloway faction may have had some effect in Philadelphia, but progress made toward nonimportation was certainly the more important factor in maintaining the tranquility of the city, as least so far as the mechanics were concerned. The impatient radical Charles Thomson's analysis of the non-importation decision reveals that there was little consensus for —even if there was no violence against—the "politics of ingratiation" in 1765: "So exasperated are the People," he wrote, "that to appease them and indeed for our own Safety the merchants are obliged to pawn their word and honor and give under their hands that they will not import any more Goods from Great Britain until that act is repealed."[24]

The Quakers could not have kept the lid on had not a shadow government developed which both spoke to the interests of, and incorporated the leadership elements within, the mechanic community.[25] It is a mistake to extrapolate from the evidence about the White Oaks—an organization of mechanics in the building trades, who were very different from the main body of artisans in that they were unaffected by market competition from abroad—to reach the conclusion that urban artisans were, as a community, conservative partisans of the Quaker faction, and that this phenomenon preserved the peace in Philadelphia during 1765. Peace there was, but it was founded on non-importation.

If mechanics were bound to neither of the principal factions in Pennsylvania's complicated political structure, there remains the question of their relations with emerging extra-legal political organizations. One of the most persistent myths of American history is that disadvantaged and dispossessed classes—farmers in the countryside and mechanics and other laboring classes in the cities— used the occasion of the various protests against imperial policy to launch battles of their own—to determine "who should rule at home."[26] Philadelphia's history during the Stamp Act crisis clearly belies this notion, and the city's history throughout the decade before Independence contradicts the oversimplified "internal revolution" theory. Although most mechanics were probably more radical than most merchants (in the sense of preferring more precipitant action), their political and economic aims do not appear to have gone beyond non-importation itself. Mechanics may not have been men of wealth, but they *were* men of property—independent manufacturing entrepreneurs—and insofar as public policy concomitantly advanced their economic interests and protested the unconstitutional tax, they had no reason to wish further protest. Had there not been an extra-legal alternative to Pennsylvania's preoccupied Assembly, or had merchants failed to follow the recommendations of the Stamp Act Congress, or had merchants rescinded their compact before repeal of the Stamp Act, mechanics probably would have acted independently and more stridently to promote their cause. For this is precisely what happened only a few years later.

The crisis precipitated by Charles Townshend's Revenue Acts began much as the Stamp Act crisis had begun. The Assembly's myopic vision still focused on its old program to transfer the government from the Penn family to the Crown, and it tried its best to ignore the Townshend legislation, arguing that non-importation or other vehement protest measures would be "premature and highly imprudent, till the petition of the colonies to the King and Parliament shall have been presented."[27] Philadelphia's close corporate government politely acknowledged the crisis, but contended that although "public" measures might be appropriate in Boston, they were not in Philadelphia.[28] Some progress had been made in the sphere of legal politics: the loyalty of the two principal political factions to the home government—the Quaker because it was still practicing the "politics of ingratiation," and the Proprietary because of traditional allegiances reinforced by the recent rebuff of the Assembly's Privy Council petition in 1765—forced those opposed to ministerial policies to form a new party. In mid-1766, the men who had played leadership roles in development of effective extra-legal protest against the Stamp Act in 1765 created the Presbyterian or Whig Party.[29] Notwithstanding this development, however, political opposition in 1768 and 1769 would have to be extra-legal. The new party had been slow to develop a strong constituency, and it was working against a well-entrenched and superbly organized Quaker Party, which not only controlled the political establishment but was also active, as it had been in 1765, in attempting to quell overt demonstrational activity.[30]

In extra-legal politics, however, the forces against non-importation were more formidable than they had been in 1765.[31] The powerful "dry goods" merchants (those trading primarily with England) pointed out that non-importation was discriminatory because they suffered the entire economic burden while the "wet goods" merchants (trading with the West Indies and Wine Islands) were permitted to carry on business unimpeded.[32] Some merchants who believed non-importation should be the concern only of those who imported, resisted the movement because they believed the strongest proponents of trade boycott were not merchants but mechanics.[33] In this they may have been correct. "A Tradesman," writing in the *Pennsylvania Chronicle,* complained that the importation of British goods was the source of poverty, idleness, pride, "and a crowd of vices arising from there," and recommended that artisans follow the example of New York mechanics by refusing to buy imported goods, even if the merchants were too selfish to restrict importation themselves: "The remedy of these mischiefs lies intirely in our power, if we can firmly resolve to purchase none of these destructive articles. The general concurrence will make any instance of contrary practice disreputable and shameful, and the merchants will soon leave off importing them."[34]

The views of mechanics were, of course, not the only pressures being brought to bear on Philadelphia's merchant community. Colonists throughout the continent encouraged Philadelphia to adopt a non-importation policy, because it was obvious to everyone that a boycott could not be effective unless all major cities participated.[35] Eventually these arguments won the day in Philadelphia and an agreement was signed in February–March of 1769.

Although dry goods merchants were probably always reluctant patriots, they remained "steady to their Agreement" throughout 1769.[36] An efficient policing of maritime activity by a special merchants' committee satisfied them that their competitors would be unable to cheat, even if many suspected that merchants in other cities were importing vast quantities of English goods under various loopholes.[37] Some, in fact, apparently found ways to profit by the conditions created by non-importation. In early 1770, one anonymous tradesman "of some standing" declared that he and "thousands

of others who are living by the sweat of our brows . . . find it a
difficult matter now to subsist with reputation" because a few merchants had monopolized and inflated prices of certain essential
goods. He threatened to expose and publicly censure the wrong-
doers.[38] We do not know whether the threat was carried out, but its
articulation reveals that there was little harmony on the subject of
non-importation in Philadelphia.

However unhappy they may have been with the non-importation compact, it is unlikely that the dry goods merchants could have
done much about it during 1769. The measure carried widespread
public support, which would have been difficult to crack. For example in July, the arrival of a shipload of malt consigned to the
merchant Amos Strettle, but apparently not ordered by him, drew
the attention of the merchants' committee: recognizing that this attempt to undermine the agreement could be advantageously used
to display (and influence) public opinion, the committee called a
general meeting of the inhabitants to "take Advice on this present
Occasion." At the meeting, the city's brewers "attended in a Body,
with an Agreement which they had drawn up and signed, wherein
they engage, that as the Load of Malt just arrived was shipped contrary to the Agreement of Merchants and Traders, they will not purchase any Part of it; nor will they brew the same, or any Part
thereof, for any Person whatever."[39]

This kind of well-managed public support made it virtually
impossible for the merchants to stage an overt attempt to overthrow
the non-importation agreement in the early months. But during the
winter of 1769–70 they began organizing themselves for a repeal
drive.[40] What the embattled dry goods importers needed was a reasonable excuse for putting their plans into action, and this Parliament mercifully provided in the spring of 1770. When news arrived
in Philadelphia that all the Townshend duties except the one on tea
had been repealed, dry goods merchants moved quickly to undo non-
importation (except on tea). But the manufacturing community
found its voice. On May 7, the *Pennsylvania Chronicle* carried an
unsigned article which inquired "Whether (in case the Merchants
break through their Resolutions of Non-Importation) it will not be
high Time for the Farmers and Tradesmen to resolve, that they will

not buy any Goods from them, which in any Manner shall interfere with the Manufactures of this Province."[41]

Before May of 1770, mechanics had often formed associations for various purposes and they had often spoken out on the public issues of the day which affected them; yet these associations were confined to single crafts or small groups of crafts, and had been primarily concerned with legislative lobbying or non-political purposes. During 1765 and 1766, mechanics participated in extra-legal public affairs, but it was not necessary for them to organize separately because merchants themselves provided leadership for an extra-legal movement whose chief result was public policy which protected home manufacturers. But in May of 1770, it became apparent that tradesmen could count on neither the legally constituted government nor the existing extra-legal association. Departing radically from traditional reliance on merchant leadership, mechanics organized a public meeting of their own to deal with the crisis situation. It agreed upon a five-point program:

1. to maintain non-importation "by all prudential ways and means";
2. to "exert our Influence for the Promotion of American Manufactures, both by using them ourselves, and by recommending them to others";
3. to boycott any merchant who might break the agreement;
4. to establish a policy of non-intercourse with Rhode Island, which had broken its non-importation agreement; and
5. to attend a meeting (scheduled for June 5) of the non-importation subscribers to demand continuation of the compact.[42]

The merchants who had covenanted to suspend importation in 1769 had always regarded the agreement as their private affair, and they were offended and angry at the idea (point 5 of the mechanics' program) that their sphere of responsibility might be invaded.[43] "A Lover of Liberty and a Mechanic's Friend" reported that some merchants in town had declared that *"Mechanics* have no *Right* to give their sentiments respecting an importation," and that the tradesmen were "A Rabble."[44] But there was little the merchants could do to stop the sudden momentum the artisans had gained. The mechanics had a powerful constitutional argument which they used effectively to rebut the "*small, selfish* Merchants [who] warmly contend for an Importation of every Article of British Manufacture, except Tea."[45] A continuation of non-importation would "have a Tendency to Settle the Dispute about the Right of Taxation" and would "obtain the *glorious Object of our Struggles, American Liberty,* upon constitutional and commercial Principles."[46] Such questions ought not to be decided by one small segment of the community: "I hope every freeman, whether he be a farmer, merchant, or mechanick," wrote one newspaper correspondent, "will insist upon his right to a vote in so important an affair."[47] Against such arguments, the merchants had little hope of excluding the mechanics and other Philadelphians from a role in the decision as to whether to continue non-importation.

Although they could not exclude mechanics, the dry goods merchants were determined to make them as uncomfortable as possible at the June 5 meeting. They made it plain that they resented the introduction of "the body of disaffected Mechanics," contending that "their Consultations should be free, and not subject to any Constraint."[48] In the course of the meeting, one manufacturer apparently influenced the proceedings in a way contrary to the interests of the dry goods merchants, for which he was publicly chided both at the meeting and in the public prints.[49] But "A House Carpenter" defended the troublemaker, emphasizing that this individual had "laid out large sums to promote a valuable manufactory in this city, which every lover of America wishes may prosper." His defense carefully isolated the economic issue which separated mechanics and merchants: the merchants, he said, "dread a further continuance of the non-importation agreement, as [they] see with grief and astonishment that if they continue one year longer the vend for British manufactures will be ruined in future, as industry, manufacturing and economy gain ground every hour, which will finally render English goods unnecessary."[50] Certainly this was an over-statement of the case, but it does indicate both the fears and the expectations which this trade boycott created in the minds of Philadelphians.

To the consternation of many dry goods merchants, the June 5 meeting resolved to continue the non-importation policy.[51] We have no way of knowing whether it was the presence of the mechanics which made the decision possible. Charles Thomson, who John Adams later described as "the Sam. Adams of Philadelphia—the life of the Cause of Liberty, they say," had been carrying on an extensive campaign for over a month to prevent alteration of the compact, a campaign which included publication of an influential letter from Benjamin Franklin, the colony's agent in London, urging continuation of non-importation until all the Revenue Acts had been repealed.[52] The fact that the mechanics' side was victorious in the first round of the controversy is less important, however, than the fact that it was the occasion for the artisan community to establish itself as a political force in Philadelphia. The change in the mechanics' posture during the spring of 1770 is one of the most striking events in the history of Philadelphia in the eighteenth century. Previously, they had been temperate and cooperative, and their demands had been modest because, in the absence of responsive governmental action, the extra-legal political bodies had adopted policies with which they were in fundamental agreement. But in May of 1770, it became apparent to them that they would have to strike out on their own if they were to obtain what they wanted.

Although the tradesmen had won the vote at the June 5 meeting, they recognized that the votes on the other side were so numerous and of such weight that they could no longer count on the kind of consensus that had prevailed in 1769 to keep the dry goods merchants honest. So they formed their own "Mechanicks Committee." Late in June, when reports circulated that a few merchants had landed goods from a Glasgow ship in violation of the non-importation compact, it was announced that "Their conduct is . . . under the inspection of the Merchants Committee, to whom if the Delinquints dont make ample satisfaction, they will be dealt with by the Mechanicks Committee."[53]

Despite the efforts of non-importation proponents, it became increasingly difficult, as the summer of 1770 elapsed, to restrain merchants who wished to alter the agreement. The chief argument for rescinding centered on developments in other colonies. For several years, Philadelphians had watched apprehensively as Baltimore grew in size and importance, siphoning off much of Philadelphia's trade with the Pennsylvania backcountry,[54] and against this back-ground Baltimore's decision to revoke its non-importation agreement, giving the Chesapeake merchants a free hand in their diversion of trade with the region west of the Susquehanna, had a powerful impact on Philadelphia. This development, together with the combined betrayals of Boston, Newport, and New York, gave great momentum to the forces promoting an alteration in the boycott agreement.[55] One hundred thirty-five of the three hundred merchants who had signed the 1769 non-importation agreement met on September 20 at Josiah Davenport's tavern where they rejected the notion that non-importation was a matter of general public concern and voted to alter the agreement, confining it to tea alone.[56] Although the Davenport meeting did not represent a majority of the non-importation subscribers, public consensus no longer stood against merchants who wished to resume trade. Riding on the crest of their success, they taunted their opponents: "The Dry Goods Merchants conceive, that their adopting the Plan not to import the Articles subject to a Duty [tea] . . . ought to be strengthened by the Importers of Wine, Molasses, Coffee &c *who* wholly support the American Revenue, with the Board of Commissioners, and the numerous Train of officers dependent upon them."[57]

The mechanics and radical merchants had boycotted the Davenport meeting on the grounds that it was not called by the merchants' executive committee; after the meeting the executive committee resigned and the entire anti-Davenport group roundly denounced the desertion of the dry goods merchants.[58] "A Tradesman" wrote that since questions of public welfare and liberty were central to non-importation, "the Consent of the Majority of the Tradesmen, Farmers and other Freemen . . . should have been obtained."[59] "A Citizen" declared: "Let the Powers of Patriotism be drawn from their *proper Source*. Let the Landlords, artificers, and independent Freemen of this Province, take upon themselves the Defense of these Liberties in which they have the greatest and most substantial interest."[60] At the first public meeting after the Davenport decision, four mechanics were elected to a new extra-legal committee (composed primarily of the members of the former merchants' executive committee) appointed to propagate the citizens' denunciation of the Davenport betrayal.[61]

Notwithstanding the intense efforts of mechanics and radical merchants to keep the issue quick, non-importation very rapidly lost its public support after the summer of 1770. Organized political activity among mechanics, however, was far from dead. The latent force which Alexander Graydon later called the "mechanical interest" was awakened during that summer and remained active in Philadelphia politics for the balance of the Revolutionary era.[62] Moreover, before long it was expressing itself in legal as well as extra-legal political affairs.

Mechanics in the Ascendency, 1770-74

UNTIL 1770, mechanics as a community had not been much concerned with the two political bodies which formally governed the city—the Philadelphia Corporation and the Pennsylvania Assembly. The corporation was a close, self-perpetuating, elitist government, insulated from the daily social concerns of Philadelphians. It was a medieval institution, clearly unsuited to the demands of a dynamic, modern metropolis, and it was for this reason that a series of independent annually elected agencies—tax assessors and collectors, street commissioners, wardens (to manage the night watch and street lighting), overseers of the poor—were invented by the Assembly to perform essential civic tasks.[1]

Mechanics seldom held public office in Philadelphia before the Revolutionary era. They were never chosen to sit in the Common Council (from which members of the Board of Aldermen and the Mayor were selected), and they offered themselves for elective offices in Philadelphia city and county only rarely. For the most part, Philadelphia was a well-regulated city, and mechanics had no special motive for seeking office. Moreover, they were regular participants in private agencies, such as fire and library companies, which performed many essential civic services.

Beginning at about 1770, however, the tradesmen began to take a new attitude toward their local government. In 1769, there had been a row about street-paving, some of the poorer citizens claiming that the streets commonly used by them—especially the back lanes and alleys—were given low priority when pavement was laid, while the expensive residential sections not only received earlier paving but also the services of the city's scavenger.[2] Many Philadelphians, including mechanics, began to discover reasons for becoming more directly involved in the local political process.[3] This awakening coincided with the mechanics' rather sudden emergence as a separate force in extra-legal politics. Perhaps it was inevitable that the flame kindled in one area would spread to the other. Robert Kennedy, engraver and copper plate printer, recognized the changing mood among tradesmen and structured a campaign for sheriff of Philadelphia city and county around it in 1770: "Tho' I am the first Mechanic who, for a series of Years, has applied for this Office," he said to the mechanics in the electorate, "I am Confident of your Favors."[4] Three years later, the death of the Philadelphia coroner, Caleb Cash (who had been re-elected to the county office annually since 1764), opened the position, and there were seven candidates, three of whom were tradesmen.[5] Another artisan ran for sheriff the same year.[6] No mechanic was elected county sheriff or county coroner until after the War for Independence, but this is less significant than the fact that they began to seek the offices.

Tradesmen were more successful in obaining office when the electorate was restricted to the city. Before 1770, an average of less than three mechanics were elected to the ten commission seats (two wardens, two street commissioners, and six tax assessors and collectors); but in 1770 and 1771, four were chosen; in 1772, six; in 1773, seven; and in 1774 and 1775, eight.[7] The political awareness among artisans which was generated in the non-importation struggle was spilling over into municipal politics.

The same pattern appears in mechanics' attitude toward and participation in provincial politics. Before 1770, artisans had little interest in the Assembly. Like most eighteenth-century communities, Philadelphia deferred the mysteries of governing to men of wealth, education, and breeding. Mechanics occasionally appeared as supplicants before the legislature, and they were usually disappointed and angry about the short shrift they received there, but this political participation involved isolated issues, such as the ropemakers' demand for regulation of hemp dealers. The manufacturing community as a whole never made a general demand for responsive and responsible representation in the Assembly. One reason for this is that for the most part the Assembly was a benevolent governing body from mechanics' point of view: it was the Assembly, for example, which created the independent commissions to perform civic functions ignored by the city corporation; it was the Assembly which provided funds for the commissions to carry out the improvement and modernization of the city; and it was the Assembly which sponsored legislation, such as currency bills, designed to advance the commercial economy of Philadelphia in which mechanics were so deeply involved.

Mechanics' lack of participation in city politics before 1770 had nothing to do with the question of franchise qualifications. Contrary to historical myth, most manufacturers probably were able to vote.[8] The property qualification for the franchise was £50; that is, the voter had to testify that he owned a freehold or taxable personal property valued at £50. The tools alone owned by many master mechanics were probably sufficient to pass the franchise test; many journeymen may even have held sufficient personal property to qualify to vote. Thomas Paine once observed that a Pennsylvanian could usually qualify for the vote if he owned "a chest of tools, a few implements of husbandry, a few spare clothes, a bed and a few household utensils, a few articles for sale in a window, or almost anything else he could call or even think his own."[9]

Paine's final remark was not made in jest. Franchise tests were seldom rigidly enforced, and unless challenged, a citizen whose claim to ownership of sufficient property was doubtful—or even fraudulent—might vote for years without being found out. Only in rare and closely contested elections was there careful "Scrutinizing into the Quality of those who offered to Vote."[10]

Artisans themselves never doubted that they could vote. A week after the Davenport betrayal in September of 1770, "A Brother Chip" rallied his "Bretheren the Tradesmen, Mechanics, &c. the *useful* and *necessary* Inhabitants of this Province," complaining that a "Company of leading Men" had traditionally nominated all the candidates for office in Philadelphia,

> without ever permitting the affirmative or negative Voice of a Mechanic to interfere, and when they have concluded, expect Tradesmen will give a Sanction thereto by passing the Ticket; this we have tamely submitted to so long, that those Gentlemen make no Scruple to say, that the Mechanics (though by far the most numerous, especially in this County) have no Right to *speak* or *think* for themselves. But I would beg Leave to ask, have we not the same Privileges and Liberties to preserve or lose as themselves? Have we not an equal Right of electing, or being elected? If we have not the Liberty of nominating such Persons whom we approve, our Freedom of voting is at an End. . . . I would not be understood that we should unite to oppose them, but with them, in chusing upright Men, who will promote the public Good; at the same Time I think it absolutely necessary, that one or two Mechanics be elected to represent so large a Body of the Inhabitants.[11]

This is one of the most revealing paragraphs ever written by a mechanic in the period before the War. It indicates (1) that mechanics normally were possessed of the franchise; (2) that heretofore they had not exercised the power latent in their voting strength, and had deferred to merchants and lawyers; (3) that the traditional deference was being called into question and tradesmen were demanding a responsible government in which the manufacturing constituency was heeded; and (4) that their aim was not to oppose or destroy the existing government, but to join with others at the helm of state. There can be no question that in 1770 the artisans were expanding their political power, but there can also be no question that they considered it both possible and desirable to exercise that power within the established system. It was a very temperate brand of radicalism they espoused.

No other writer at the time disagreed with "A Brother Chip" when he concluded that his program could be realized by "Our present excellent Mode of voting by Ballot."[12] Others apparently shared Chip's assumption that mechanics possessed the franchise in

sufficient quantity to affect local and provincial politics if they chose
to. The reply to Chip which appeared the next week in William
Goddard's *Chronicle,* for example, denounced the attempt "to per-
suade the good people of this province, to chuse mechanics to represent them at the ensuing election," but did not challenge the assumption that tradesmen did have the powers of electing and being
elected.[13] Joseph Galloway made the same assumption when he
wrote Franklin with some alarm that "the White Oaks and Mechanics or many of them have left the old Ticket."[14]

Galloway's concern was well founded. The demands of "A
Brother Chip," coming on the heels of the dramatic entrance of
mechanics on the extra-legal political stage and the disintegration of
the Quaker Party's campaign to royalize the colony, was having a
powerful impact on leaders of the Dickinson faction.[15] The emergent
political organization—the faction corresponding to the anti-
Davenport merchants—drew up a ticket for Philadelphia county
assemblymen in1770 to oppose the "old corrupt Junto"; it included
Joseph Parker, a successful artisan tailor, who was among three
members of the ticket elected.[16] It is apparent that when tradesmen
demanded an "equal right to agreements and resolutions with others
for the public good," they meant the injunction to apply to the
colony's legal political system as well as its extra-legal governing
bodies.[17]

The new presence of mechanics in the political establishment
was no more pleasing to those who had traditionally ruled the roost
than the inroads made by craftsmen in extra-legal affairs had been.
The election of Parker, for example, resulted in "Many Threats,
Reflections, Sarcasms and Burlesques" being "thrown out" against
mechanics.[18] But the acrimony did not deter the tradesmen. They
recognized that as the Revolutionary crisis deepened, the conservativism of the provincial Assembly was becoming more damaging to
their interests. The extra-legal committee structure provided a safety
valve which absorbed political extremities in such a way that neither
mechanics nor other radicals felt impelled to overturn the legal
governmental system, but at the same time there was a growing
awareness in Philadelphia that unless the traditional political structure could be brought into the conflict over fundamental imperial

policies, Pennsylvania would be impotent. This may explain artisans' accelerating interest in the electoral process.

A curious episode involving Philadelphia's most skillful artisan printer is illustrative of the emerging attitudes of mechanics. William Goddard, of Rhode Island, had been brought to the city in 1766 by the leadership of the Quaker Party, Joseph Galloway and Thomas Wharton, with the object of establishing a press sympathetic to their views.[19] William Bradford, printer of the *Pennsylvania Journal,* was an old and vigorous enemy of Galloway, and the partnership of David Hall and Benjamin Franklin, publisher of the *Pennsylvania Gazette,* had dissolved in 1766, whereupon this paper, too, began to oppose Galloway.[20] The new printer may not have fully perceived his secret partners' political sentiments or intentions when he came to the city (they had asked only that he print an unbiassed paper), but he soon developed a bitter enmity for them. When Galloway and Wharton discovered that Goddard's idea of a free press included publication of Dickinson's *Letters from a Farmer in Pennsylvania* (the *Chronicle* was the first to publish them, which was extra salt in the wound), they made every effort to quash the printer and his journal.[21] They got more than they bargained for: Goddard's campaign against Galloway forced the powerful speaker of the Assembly to seek election in Bucks County, rather than Philadelphia where he had formerly led the Quaker ticket. Mechanics lost out to dry goods merchants in late September when the Davenport meeting rescinded non-importation, but Goddard led them to a sweet revenge in the humiliation of Galloway at the Philadelphia polls in early October. The artisan printer projected his invective over several years, and in 1772 he was so successful that he was very nearly spontaneously elected himself.[22] Shy deference was a thing of the past in the political thinking of Philadelphia's artisans.

Political activity in the manufacturing community began in the city's extra-legal committee structure in 1768 because mechanics recognized that the most effective strategy was to circumvent the lethargic Assembly. Before long, however, extra-legal committees, and the public meetings which authorized them, were not only acting in the Assembly's stead, but also prodding and attacking the legislature itself.[23] One citizen reported in 1768 that "town-meetings (in imitation of the orderly republicans of Boston) have lately become a popular device for giving instructions" to the Assembly.[24] By 1772, the idea that the people had a right to instruct and criticize their representatives in the colonial legislature was firmly established. For example, when a new excise tax on liquor was enacted it was venomously attacked by a public meeting in which Philadelphia mechanics were prominent and which was chaired by an artisan fishing-tackle-maker.[25] They protested that it was a partial tax because the incidence would fall with greatest severity on "the middling and poorer Class of the inhabitants," and they denounced it as anti-libertarian because it authorized "unconstitutional" searches and seizures.[26] Having condemned the tax, the assemblage of inhabitants took swipes at other activities of the Assembly with which it disagreed, including the Leather Act, "in particular [because] it oppresses the Poor, by Shoes being considerably advanced in Price."[27]

So intense was political activity within the artisan community that a new organization was born to campaign for political candidates and propagate the demands of the mechanics. The Patriotic Society, according to its Articles, was pledged "to promote . . . and preserve, inviolate, our just Rights and Privileges, to us and our Posterity, against every Attempt to violate the same, either here or on the other side of the Atlantic."[28] One apologist for the Society revealed that the focus of its activities would be the provincial elections: "experience proves, that the very men whom you entrust with the support and defense of your most sacred liberties, are frequently corrupt, not only in *England* but also in the Colonies. . . . If ever therefore your rights are preserved, it must be through the virtue and integrity of the middling sort of people, as farmers, tradesmen, &c. who despise venality, and best know the sweets of liberty."[29]

There was, in short, some intense class-related feeling at work in Philadelphia by 1772. Both the Patriotic Society and the public meeting called to protest the excise tax stopped short of advocating revolution, for there is no evidence that mechanics envisioned overturning either the government or the method of electing it. But they did believe the record of some of the Assembly's incumbents did not warrant their re-election. "Publius" was specific as to the reason why: the Assembly had made expenditures for public roads which

were for "private emolument," not the public good; it had enacted
the excise law, which was more "iniquitous" than similar oppressive
laws in England; and it had passed the Leather Act, "from which
no advantage can arise."[30]

It was deferential politics, not discriminatory franchise laws,
that mechanics and their organizations strove to overcome in the
years before Independence. They were, one said, "determined for
the future, at every election, to scrutinize and inspect into the character and proceedings of our delegates."[31] With the idea in mind of
keeping a more careful watch on the Assembly, mechanics attacked
"the absurd and tyrranical custom of shutting the Assembly doors"
during debates.[32] "A Citizen of Philadelphia" suggested to mechanics that they demand to know what their assemblymen had actually
done on their behalf during the past year before returning them to
office.[33] The lesson learned during the extra-legal struggle over non-
importation—that committees could act as pressure-groups on the
legislature—and the lesson learned in the election of 1770—that
mechanics acting as a unified body could affect the electoral process
—were brought together in the Patriotic Society, which was a
comprehensive organization, devoted to both campaigning and
lobbying.[34]

The presence of the Patriotic Society made Philadelphia's politics quite lively in 1773. One observer commented that some Philadelphians were saying " 'It is Time the Tradesmen were checked' "
—" 'They take too much upon them' "—" 'They ought not to inter-
meddle in State Affairs' "—" 'They will become too powerful.' "[35]
Another noted that the Galloway faction had been "plotting the ruin
of their Country, disturbing the Repose of Society, and abusing every
Man, particularly the members of the *Patriotic Society,* who would
not bow the Knee to the Image they had set up."[36] Yet another, styled
"Pacificus," remarked on the lack of "Decency, Unanimity and Harmony" in the election campaign, to which "A Mechanic" returned
the following abrasive reply:

> Pacificus . . . views with Anguish of Soul the growing Interest
> and Importance of the Worthy Mechanics and Manufacturers of
> this City, and their Friends in the Country, and . . . their Spirit

of Resolution, so vigorously exerted, at the two last Elections, was the first *shock* that removed the *Mist* from [his] Eyes. . . . Americus [Galloway] and his Junto of Conspirators against the Liberties of their Country [will soon] lose the Power they have so arrogantly assumed, of treading upon the Necks of Mechanics, and their Friends, and giving Law to this opulent City and County.[37]

This was not idle political rhetoric. "A Mechanic" urged his fellow artisans to make use of "the Means that the Constitution allows us to use for our Defense and Preservation," and suggested that they "exert themselves to the utmost, at the next Election, (when they [mechanics] will have the Power of redressing themselves in their own Hands) by choosing such Men to represent them, who have, in addition to Integrity of Heart, Heads to plan, Spirit to execute, and who can feel for such of their Constituents who stand most in need of their Care and Protection."[38]

Two incumbent assemblymen, one from the city and one from the county, both of whom were opposed by "A Mechanic," failed of re-election in 1773 (Benjamin Franklin and Samuel Miles were chosen in their places). The mechanics did not possess a controlling majority in the county or city constituencies, but they did comprise a sufficiently large segment of the population to influence election outcomes when they acted in concert. The election of 1773 proved that the program of the Patriotic Society to awaken latent political power in the artisan community was a success.

It was inevitable that the intense political activism which had transferred itself from the extra-legal sphere of politics to the electoral process would be easily transferred back again from the legal to the extra-legal. This is what occurred later in 1773 when Philadelphia confronted the Tea Act. Members of the manufacturing community declared their opinion of the tax right from the start, not waiting for merchants to take the initiative, and making it plain they would not be persuaded by the argument that trade boycotts were the private business of the traders: "Let us not be prevailed upon to suppose this [Act] will affect the Merchants only . . . it will also very materially affect . . . every member of the community."[39]

Throughout the fall and early winter, "Anxiety and Suspense" gripped the city, for no one was quite sure how the protest would register itself.[40] Thomas Wharton wrote that "threats are throw'd out . . . ; to such a pitch of Zeal are some People rais'd that, I fear the Worst."[41] The merchants to whom the East-India Company's tea had been consigned were forced to "renounce all Pretensions to execute that commission" by a new extra-legal committee.[42]

Philadelphia avoided violence during the Tea Act crisis because its committee prevented the tea ship bound for the city from reaching its destination. When the ship entered the Delaware, a deputation rode down to Gloucester Point, where the ship was hailed and her captain brought overland to Philadelphia to be acquainted with the people's firm resolution against the landing of his cargo. The captain was instructed immediately to provision his ship for a return voyage to England. Wary of the seething tempers in town, he set sail the next day.[43] Philadelphia turned away its tea without incident, but Boston did not, and Parliament's retributive legislation against the Bostonians precipitated a new political crisis in Pennsylvania.

Mechanics and radical merchants believed the logical form of protest in this new imperial crisis was another trade boycott, this time combining non-importation with non-exportation and non-consumption. The arguments favoring trade boycott made as much or more sense in 1774 as they had in 1765 and 1768–69. At the same time, however, the dry goods merchants who hated non-importation in 1765 and 1768–69 detested the idea of non-intercourse and nonconsumption in 1774. They resented the fact that they would be forced to "risque their whole property, while others are totally exempted from any risque."[44] When Paul Revere rode into town on May 19 with a letter from Boston radicals asking for Philadelphia's support in their opposition to parliamentary tyranny, factions of every persuasion began mobilizing for a public meeting scheduled for the next day at City Tavern.[45] Charles Thomson, Joseph Reed, and Thomas Mifflin, the moderate leadership, knew that mechanics and other radicals would press for an unequivocal commitment to non-importation, and they also knew that it would be difficult to obtain a consensus in favor of this policy, so powerful were the dry goods merchants. Therefore, although they ultimately favored non-intercourse, they attempted "to place the offensive Object in an oblique View" by obtaining a commitment merely to elect an extra-legal committee which would send a "friendly and affectionate reply to Boston and take steps to have delegates to a continental congress chosen."[46]

As Charles Thomson put it,

> To press matters was the sure way of cementing that union [of forces opposed to trade boycott protests] and thereby raising a powerful party in the State against the Cause of America, whereas by prudent management and an improvement of occurrences as they happened there was reason to hope that the Assembly, and consequently the whole Province, might be brought into the dispute without any considerable opposition.[47]

It was a delicate strategy, requiring the assistance of the man "in the highest point of reputation and possessed [of] a vast influence," namely, John Dickinson, with whom Reed, Thomson, and Mifflin conspired to manipulate the May 20 City Tavern meeting.[48]

The meeting of May 20 was "composed of all ranks and interests" in the city. According to Thomson's narrative, Mifflin and Reed suggested radical measures which precipitated a "Great clamour" and debate, at which point Dickinson proposed a compromise —to reply to Boston and appoint a Committee, but not to adopt a non-intercourse policy until a continental congress had considered it—which was accepted.[49] Two tickets for committee were then proposed, and the debate again warmed, but Thomson moved the two tickets be combined and the entire group appointed as a single committee, which was accepted.[50] Thomson later claimed that the moderates' political engineering kept the appearance of unanimity among the people, "tempering immoderate zeal, giving time to prepare the public mind, and suffering matters to ripen gradually."[51] He was probably correct in this judgment, for it is unlikely that a consensus could have been mustered for a more radical position at the City Tavern meeting. The mechanics, however, did not share Thomson's patience.

The mechanics thought the letter composed by the May 20 committee to the beleaguered Bostonians was "too cold," and they were not content with the motions being made to get delegates appointed to an inter-Colonial congress.[52] The committee had asked the governor to convene the Assembly (which would then appoint the delegates), but the governor refused the request on June 8, and the same day a broadside appeared calling for a meeting of the mechanics the next day.[53]

The June 9 meeting of mechanics must have been a stormy one. Twelve hundred tradesmen assembled in the State House yard and listened to the reading of a radical communication from New York mechanics, as well as other papers.[54] Not wishing to trust public affairs to the mild-tempered May 20 Committee (composed almost entirely of merchants), the mechanics appointed their own committee "to co-operate with the Committee of merchants, and to strengthen their hands, and to form such resolutions, as will convince the world Americans were born and determined to live free."[55]

Again mechanics stopped short of political extremity—their committee was charged to "cooperate" and "strengthen," not to undermine and overthrow—but their forceful voices threw a scare into the moderate leadership. The May 20 committee, anticipating trouble from the June 9 mechanics' meeting, sent a delegation to it which announced a new public meeting, hinted that "Resolves big with uncommon Wisdom & Spirit" would be proposed, and promised the appointment of "one grand joint Committee to represent the whole inhabitants of this city and county."[56]

The calling of a new public meeting touched off a fresh round of manuevering by the various factions in the city. The first tactic adopted by the moderates was to delay the meeting a few days. It was originally scheduled for 3:00 P.M. on June 15, a Wednesday, a time when mechanics and other radicals from the city could easily attend; it was put off until 3:00 P.M. on June 18, a Saturday, in order to accommodate the more moderate farmers from outside the city who would be coming to market.[57] Moderates hoped the farmers would tranquilize radical enthusiasm among mechanics.

A second tactic in the moderates' continuing political engineering was to call a closed meeting of delegates "from *all* Societies in Town, to devise, consult, and deliberate upon Propostions, to be laid before the Grand Meeting of Inhabitants."[58] It was a carefully rigged caucus, which coopted the hesitant Quaker leadership by involving it in the planning process.[59] Moderate leaders convinced the group to sponsor three propositions: (1) a resolution declaring the Boston Port Bill to be oppressive to American liberties; (2) a commitment to deal with the emergency through the aegis of a continental congress; and (3) an opinion that the Assembly would be the most "eligible" agency for choosing delegates to the congress, or if that proved impossible, that the people "in the same way they chuse representatives, elect a certain number of delegates for a provincial convention and that this convention should elect the delegates."[60]

From the mechanics' point of view, the Meeting of Societies' program was far from the "Resolves big with uncommon Wisdom & Spirit" they had been led to expect; in fact, it seemed "weak & without Spirit such that the smallest petty Town on the continent would have been ashamed of."[61] Moreover, to add insult to injury, the Meeting of Societies had proposed a slate for the new committee composed largely of the May 20 City Tavern merchants and other conservatives.[62] The taverns and street-corners buzzed, and it quickly became apparent that the meeting scheduled for June 18 was in for some real trouble.[63] The mechanics detected "Deceit & Treachery . . . concealed under the apparent Prudence of [the] Resolves; and they were "prepared to reject the Men, who were the cause of such shameful Delays . . . and who had the Influence to carry such weak timid & deceitful Resolves in the [Meeting of Societies]."[64]

Moderates knew they were caught in a dangerous vise. Mechanics were exerting tremendous pressure from the left, but if they yielded, their entire program to obtain a commitment to a Continental Congress (and through it, non-intercourse) would be defeated by a powerful phalanx of conservative merchants. Desperately, they met in a secret caucus the night before the June 18 meeting "to collect their Sentiments."[65] They agreed to "abstain from all Hissing and every Motion that would tend to Affront or degrade any of our Bretheren and use our United Influence for that purpose." Secondly, they decided to remove from their ticket the names of the Reverend William Smith and Thomas Wharton, who were the two candidates most offensive to radicals. Thirdly, to mollify the dissidents, seven mechanics and six Germans were added to the slate. And fourthly, it was decided to attempt to elect the slate as a unit, rather than permitting votes on individual candidates.[66]

The June 18 meeting at the State House was tense. None were permitted to enter the yard except those enjoying the right to vote, yet still there were 8,000, by one estimate.[67] The moderate leadership prevailed upon John Dickinson to sit in the chair, which was an act of great prudence because mechanics held him in such reverence that they were persuaded "to behave with Decency," even though they were seething.[68] The proposals of the Meeting of Societies were separately debated, and were adopted, despite attempts by dissident mechanics to strengthen them.[69] Then the new committee slate was proposed, together with the decision arrived at the night before to elect the slate as a single unit. The mechanics' reaction is worth recording at length:

> We plainly saw that no Resolves, however spirited, could avail us any Thing; unless the Execution of them were committed to Men of Spirit, whom we knew to be Freemen in the Cause of Freedom and such we were determined to elect.
> But then how our Hearts heave with Indignation at the Insult! then Instead of a fair & free Election Instead of being allowed the Priviledge of Freemen and Electors, we had a List made up promiscuously of Friends and Foes obtruded upon us. We were not called up to vote for them Man by Man, no! Then we would have taken Care that such, as were not hearty in the Cause of Liberty should have met with the Repulse due to their inimical Dispositions. We must take them all, or none. We must either reject our firmest & best Friends, or else admit our most inveterate, subtile, designing and determined Enemies, Men whose political Members were always and will forever be on the Side of Power & Promotion. A Committee chosen by Sixty Persons met in a very private Manner [the June 17 secret caucus], 40 of whom must have elected themselves, were obtruded upon the Freemen of this City & County with such Marks of Contempt, as were truly humiliating.

And when we seemed determined to reject the Mode of Election, our Understandings were insulted in the grossest Manner by the arguments used to enforce the Measure, and when that failed, by three County Propositions we were reduced to the dire necessity of taking the List as it stood, or of having no Committee at all.[70]

Despite the heated protests of the mechanics, the moderates had their way, and the proposed committee slate was elected as a unit. The artisans had been soundly defeated. And yet gains had been made. They had clearly influenced the city's proceedings, even though they lost the votes that meant most to them; they had gained formal recognition as a constituency of the extra-legal committee structure, even though their votes were a minority of the whole; most of all, they had regained the momentum in extra-legal politics which had dissipated in September of 1770. Coupled with the influence they had begun to cast on the legal political structure in Philadelphia after 1770, the power which had accrued to mechanics since the beginning of the Revolutionary era had been enormous. In a matter of a few years their position in the community had been transformed. Formerly a neglected, ignored, and forgotten class, outside the pale of imperial and local economic thought, and without standing in city politics, they now enjoyed significant power and prestige in both the economic and political spheres. At the same time that the boycott mode of protest snatched local manufacturing from the periphery of Philadelphia's economic concerns, the concerted efforts of the mechanics to consolidate and expand their gains in city and provincial politics reached its apogee.

Independence and Radical Politics, 1774-76

THE posture taken by moderate Pennsylvania politicians in 1774 was not to the liking of the urban artisan community primarily because a definite commitment was not made to non-intercourse and nonconsumption. Led by some of the very men who had been elevated to the June 18 committee, mechanics took every opportunity to move Philadelphia toward more radical measures.[1] The strategy they used was to demand repeatedly that the inhabitants be called again into general assemblage. Moderates considered this program "rash" and "violent," partly because they thought it would permanently alienate conservative dry goods merchants, who were presumed to be powerful and numerous, and partly because they found public meetings inherently difficult to manage. But the tradesmen remained adamant. Scolding moderates, they declared it would be as difficult to win over the Galloway faction to non-intercourse "as to try to make them Lovers of their Country, or to give up their Prospects of rising on our Ruins. . . . In the name of Wonder where is the Rashness of adopting the only Measure which is in our Power. And as to Violence, it [non-intercourse] is the only base, which can prevent it."[2]

All parties in Philadelphia seem to have been averse to "violence," but each had a different perception of what it consisted in and how it could best be avoided. Moderate politicians wished to prevent general meetings of the inhabitants, because even after extensive planning and programming they had experienced difficulties on June 18, and the growing ire of the tradesmen promised more trouble for any future meetings of this kind. The "violence" they feared was the kind of division and anarchy that would almost surely arise if radical mechanics and conservative merchants were allowed to square off against one another. This direct confrontation of opposing views could be avoided, they believed, if a non-intercourse policy were adopted and enforced by an inter-Colonial congress, rather than by local radical committees. In the words of Charles Thomson, moderates wished to "put it out of the power of the merchants, as they had done before, to drop the opposition when interest dictated the measure."[3]

Mechanics, on the other hand, agreed that a public meeting would be the occasion for the alienation of conservatives from the cause, but they welcomed the prospect. Unless conservatives *were* read out of the extra-legal councils, they believed, a worse kind of divisiveness would occur. Should Philadelphia fail to adopt a firm posture on the trade boycott issue, spontaneous "violence" in the rank and file of the people—mob activities of the kind Boston and New York had previously experienced—could easily develop; it was, after all, the adoption of non-importation, not the machinations of the politicians, which had moved Philadelphia smoothly through the crises of 1765 and 1768–69.[4]

The artisans' first opportunity to demand a new public meeting came not long after the June 18 committee began its work. Since the governor had refused to convene the Assembly during the early summer, the June 18 committee called for a provincial convention of delegates from extra-legal county committees, whose job it would be to appoint delegates to the Continental Congress. The governor subsequently convened the Assembly, on the pretext that Indian disturbances required its attention, but the convention met anyway, for the purpose of giving "instructions" to the Assembly on the subject of the Congress, as well as to elected delegates.[5] The mechanics reasoned that these developments should be the occasion for another gathering of the inhabitants to sound the people's sentiments.[6] In a carefully worded letter to the June 18 Committee, tradesmen argued that neither the Committee nor the provincial convention had

> any powers that we know of, to instruct the delegates of this province with regard to their conduct in the approaching Congress.
> . . . It is not easy to point out all the evil Consequences that must necessarily result from Sending delegates to the Congress uninstructed with regard to the Subjects which in all human probability will be there discussed. To have the business of that August body Stopped on our Account[,] the city of Philadelphia disgraced, and every thing thrown into Confusion, are events which we hope never to see realized.[7]

The reply from the committee was firm: even if a meeting were necessary, "the shortness of the time and the particular circumstances of the Season" would not permit it. Moreover, the committee expressed its confidence in the convention's ability to instruct the Assembly with "utmost Propriety," and in the Assembly properly to instruct the delegates it would elect. The Committee's conclusion summarized the moderate position:

> we have a firm confidence that whatever the congress shall devise and recommend, will be adhered to not only by every province but by every city and County and we hope by the individuals of each province. We think it best therefore to refrain from all Meetings which may have a tendency to shew any diversity of Sentiments among ourselves. We are now happily united. We are all animated in the general cause and pursuing the constitutional Mode for obtaining redress of our grievances. Let us therefore wait the event of the Congress.[8]

Having failed to convince moderate political leaders, the tradesmen next attempted to go over the head of the Committee in a direct appeal to the public. They declared that an extensive trade boycott would not be successful unless it was unanimously supported by all the colonies, and that it was therefore essential for local inhabitants, in order to prevent backsliding in the Pennsylvania delegation, to "come to some agreement themselves or *expressly* leave it to be framed for them by Congress." Protesting that they wished not to "enter into any controversy with the Committee" (which they clearly did), the mechanics reiterated their arguments that neither the Assembly nor the convention had the power to instruct delegates to the Continental Congress.[9]

All the attempts to convene a public meeting in July failed, but the mechanics persevered nonetheless during August. Near the end of the summer, for example, a rumor circulated around town that a large quantity of English merchandise was on its way to Philadelphia, shipped by English adventurers who hoped to take advantage of the anticipated dearth which non-intercourse would cause if adopted. The June 18 committee hesitated to take a stand on the issue, claiming that its charge gave it no specific authority in such matters, whereupon "An Artisan" declared that this emergency required a new public meeting, and the appointment of "a new Committee to watch over the public welfare and to advise what ought to be done on every emergency that may happen."[10] Formerly, mechanics had asked only for a public meeting to give new authority to the June 18 committee; now they wanted a public meeting, and a new committee as well.

In the autumn of 1774, the battle lines in Philadelphia shifted somewhat. The mechanics' summer campaign to replace the June 18 committee, a moderate extra-legal body committed to the simple policy of supporting the Continental Congress (which would presumably dictate an inter-Colonial response to the imperial crisis) had failed. So had their attempts to influence the Assembly to appoint radicals to the Congress, scheduled to meet in Philadelphia in September. A note to John Dickinson from the leaders of the artisan community had earlier declared: "The People begin to assemble in companies to consult what they ought to do, if any Attempt should be made to have any of those who are obnoxious to the People appointed members of the Congress. If they are it will certainly produce a Riot, and perhaps endanger their Safety. Our intelligence is good."[11]

Notwithstanding such open threats, the Assembly not only appointed a Galloway-led conservative delegation to the Congress, it also gave those men a charge which carried no commitment to non-intercourse.[12] Since they could not expect radical leadership from the Pennsylvania delegation, mechanics launched a campaign in September to influence the Congress itself. As delegates from all over America began to assemble in the city, mechanics carried out a propaganda campaign which trumpeted the "absolute necessity" of an affirmative commitment to non-intercourse, and condemned the notion of donating "certain fixed aids" to the mother country in lieu of taxes.[13]

The lobbying activities of Philadelphia mechanics and other radicals among the gathering congressional delegates were more successful than their earlier attempts to capture the minds and imaginations of the Philadelphia citizenry. From the start, the delegates were persuaded to ignore the great conservative lawyer who headed the Pennsylvania delegation: among the very first decisions of the Congress was one to meet in Carpenters Hall, home of an artisan guild, rather than the Pennsylvania Assembly Room, as Galloway had proposed; another was to give the Congress' secretarial responsibilities to Charles Thomson, a favorite of Philadelphia's radicals and an arch-opponent of Galloway's, even though Thomson was not a member of the Pennsylvania delegation. One member of Congress reported that these decisions were "highly agreeable to the mechanics and citizens in general, but mortifying to the last degree to Mr. Galloway and his party."[14]

Since early in the summer of 1774, Philadelphia's mechanics had been increasing the political pressure, step-by-step, on the forces of conservativism in the colony, and after the Congress declared a policy of non-intercourse with England in the autumn of 1774, they made yet another demand. Philadelphia's moderate political leaders always claimed that it was beneficial for the city and county of Philadelphia to work cooperatively in extra-legal politics.[15] Although moderates said this was for the purpose of maintaining unity, it did not take mechanics long to figure out that the real reason was to counter-balance urban radicalism with the moderate temper characteristic of the Quaker and German commercial farming areas adjacent to the city [16] Now that the Continental Congress had declared a full-scale boycott, it was necessary for Philadelphia to elect a new committee (the June 18 committee not having a mandate to execute the new policy), and the radicals demanded that the city and county of Philadelphia elect separate bodies.[17] The justification was clever: moderates had often sidestepped mechanics' demands for more precipitate action by claiming that it was too difficult to bring the city and county together on short notice; radicals now used precisely the same argument for separating the city and county committees, to wit, that the "frequent and sudden" meetings which would be necessary would make it inexpedient to continue the connection between the two constituencies.[18]

Little is known about the organization of the election for the new committee, but apparently a bargain was struck: as a consession to the radical element, the city and county committees would be separated; but to head off possible radical frenzy in the ensuing election, voting would be by ballot, rather than *viva voce,* thus dampening the effect of threats and intimidation from the left, and electing would take place in several locales around the city, thus eliminating the mass hysteria which characterized large public meetings.[19] This election plan apparently had the support of the city's mechanics, for the list of twenty-four inspectors chosen to supervise the election included at least thirteen tradesmen, most of whom were part of the leadership element in the manufacturing community at the time.[20] It is noteworthy that no demands for alteration of the franchise figured in the negotiation on election policy in 1774. The instructions to the election inspectors were to supervise the polls just as they would legal elections, except that if a person should offer himself as a voter who was not known to be possessed of the franchise, they were to require, "instead of an oath, a solomn declaration upon honour, of his right to vote for Members of General Assembly, and inform him at the same time, that if it shall hereafter appear that he has declared falsly, he shall be publicly advertised in the News-papers, as having abused and insulted his distressed country."[21]

Again, mechanics and other radicals sought political power, but they did not propose striking at the traditional foundations of the political system. The normal election mode was adequate to their goal of being incorporated into the political process.

The election plan for choosing new Philadelphia committeemen resulted in a successful election from everyone's point of view. It occurred without violence or intimidation of the voters, though it was an intensely fought contest.[22] Two tickets were proposed: the radical slate was headed by the central extra-legal leadership element which had held power since 1770 (Dickinson, Thomson, Mifflin, etc.), together with others representing a broad and comprehensive cross-section of the urban population, including many who were poorer and younger than those who had previously served; the moderate ticket contained many of the names proposed by radicals, but the proportion of men from Quaker and merchant backgrounds was higher, and the average wealth and age levels were also higher.[23] The radical ticket was victorious, which must have been satisfying to mechanics since a large proportion (about 33 percent) of the new Committee of Sixty-Six was composed of mechanics.[24]

The choosing of the Committee of Sixty-Six brought to a close more than six months of turbulence in Philadelphia's extra-legal politics. The objectives of the mechanics, as defined by the political leadership of the artisan community at that time, had been substantially reached, and the unified and powerful political force within the manufacturing segment of society, born in the crisis of 1770, reached its apogee in the fall of 1774. The artisans had made two primary demands—that the colony commit itself to nonintercourse, and that the extra-legal government include them in more than token numbers—both of which were now met. Nonintercourse, with all its presumed economic and psychological benefits to home manufactures, and with all its apparent power as an instrument of protest, was in force, and since it was a policy adopted by Congress, rather than by *ad hoc* local organizations, there was little chance that unhappy dry goods merchants could rescind it unilaterally. Moreover, the city's extra-legal councils had begun to incorporate significant numbers of tradesmen, many of them the very men who had led the artisan community's attempts to force more radical and strident measures in Philadelphia earlier in the year.

Ironically, success was to some extent the undoing of the movement which had begun in the artisan community in 1770. It had been sparked by a crisis and it was sustained by opposition; so long as moderate politicians tried to keep men of radical and conservative leanings united in support of a single, ambiguously defined program with which neither extreme really agreed, and so long as tradesmen resisted this persuasion by insisting upon an overt commitment to commercial boycott, the mechanic community held together as a separate and identifiable political entity. Since, however, the general political objective of mechanics had not been to snatch the reins from existing politicians and overturn the system, but rather to join in with the traditional leadership in its manipulation of the familiar (though extra-legal) scheme, it naturally followed that when this general program was realized—and especially since it was achieved concommitantly with the implementation of the mechanics' specific policy objective (non-intercourse)—the artisan community would lose its force as an independent element in Philadelphia politics. The new Committee of Sixty-Six, elected in November of 1774, coopted the mechanics' leaders of the period 1770–74, and satisfied both their general search for a more effective political voice and their specific demand for an effective commercial boycott.

The artisan community had been unified in its political behavior for four years before November of 1774, and we can trace many of the men who provided leadership in that period to the 1774 Committee of Sixty-Six.[25] Yet there is no evidence that they succeeded in keeping a unified artisan community behind them once they made this commitment. On the contrary, the artisan community, which had matured on the fringes of the political estate, quite naturally continued to spin-off new radical spokesmen who considered themselves outside the pale of mechanic leadership currently engaged in the central political activities of the city. A spiraling process developed: new radicals appeared demanding new responses to the deepening imperial crisis, tension would be resolved by incorporating them into the political leadership, leaving room for more new men to make new radical challenges in response to increased imperial oppressions.[26]

The centripetal absorption of increasingly more radical sentiment within the extra-legal committee movement was perhaps inevitable in light of the developing intransigence of the home government and the momentum of American protest. The year 1775 was a case in point. There was a new restlessness among mechanics during the summer of that year. It was based on a sense of frustration with the protest movement. In the first place, the ministry had yielded nothing; it had met Colonial firmness with force and belligerance by sealing off Massachusetts and by provoking armed conflict in Lexington and Concord. And in the second place, the boon to home manufactures which mechanics had assumed would accompany a cessation of commercial traffic never materialized. The 1774 non-intercourse and nonconsumption policy was far more comprehensive and effective than earlier boycotts, and although it did cut off the source of imported wares it also brought the entire economy to a rather sudden and devastating halt. Henry Drinker wrote that "Business of many kinds is becoming very slack here and many of our Tradesmen, who with their Families, are not in a situation to support themselves without a steady employ, we fear are already suffering from the stagnation of Trade."[27]

Against this background, new political forces began to stir. In August of 1775, the Committee of Sixty-Six's tenure came to an end, and a new Committee of One Hundred was elected to replace it. Many of the mechanics on the Committee of One Hundred were holdovers from the Committee of Sixty-Six, but there were new members "suddenly raised to power," whose radicalism was more strident than had been known on the 1774 Committee.[28] One alarmed conservative described these new participants in extra-legal government as "needy desperate Men, who could not lose anything but might gain something by the Contest. . . . You know the Consequence of such Men among the lower sort of the Community."[29]

The successful slate in the election of August 1775—known as the "mechanicks Ticket"—sustained the broadening process which was reflected in the membership of the Committee of Sixty-Six before it: membership was more heterogeneous in terms of social and economic group and age than before.[30] More important to mechanics, the numbers of committeemen from the manufacturing community rose to at least 45 percent of the whole.[31]

Yet no sooner was this absorption of emergent radical sentiment accomplished than still other new men, more radical and more organized than their predecessors, appeared at the periphery of the Committee of One Hundred. Prominent in these groups were the mechanics. One focal point of fresh radicalism was the United Company of Philadelphia for Promoting American Manufactures, an organization founded by radical mechanics in 1775 to manufacture war materiel, mainly textiles.[32] Another source was the Pennsylvania militia, formed in 1775 after Lexington and Concord. In the autumn of 1775, a group of extreme radicals calling themselves the Committee of Privates asked the enlisted men of each neighborhood militia organization to send three delegates to a meeting which would consider the efficacy of articles of association recommended by the officer corps.[33] There was an obvious leveling cast to this organization which presumed to judge and criticize on behalf of the common man; moreover, inasmuch as the officer corps was closely identified with the extra-legal committee structure, the privates' organization represented an extreme radical challenge to the authority of existing political machinery. The Committee of Privates represented a new voice in the community, speaking for men of little consequence and meager circumstances, and its leaders included several mechanics, who, like the men they led, were relatively obscure and inconsequential.[34] Samuel Simpson, characterized by one who despised him as "a drunken shoemaker," was chairman of the Committee; the Privates' Committee of Correspondence included Frederick Hagener, tailor, Edward Ryves, paper-hanger, and Robert Bell, engraver and book-binder—none of whom had ever before played a role in the affairs of the artisan community.[35]

During 1776, extra-legal political leadership began to focus on four men, a quadrumvirate who engineered a radical democratic revolution at mid-year. Two of these four had direct ties with tradesmen: one was Thomas Paine, an erstwhile stay-maker recent emigrated to America, whose artisan background undoubtedly gave him entre into the community of mechanics; the other was Timothy Matlack, a beer-brewer who had no previous political background except possibly an involvement in the brewers' boycott of 1770 and a place on the 1775 Committee of One Hundred.[36] In February of 1776 a few of the more moderate mechanics on the Philadelphia

Committee failed of re-election, and a score of new artisans—most of them previously unknown to the city's politics—were elected.[37] Once again, a committee election reflected a perceptible radical shift in Philadelphia's extra-legal politics. Moreover, the old radical leadership had been eroded by virtue of many of its strongest men being siphoned off into national politics, leaving Philadelphia to the newest and most inexperienced and most radical politicians.[38]

Because there was so little unity of concern among artisans in these years, it is difficult to generalize about their behavior. Yet the constant appearance of new mechanic faces beside the old in the increasingly radical political bodies indicates that a new force was welling up in the manufacturing community. It was natural that it should find expression in the Revolutionary committees. From the beginning of the era, mechanics had entered politics through the extra-legal committee structure, even though they possessed substantial franchise power in regular city elections. The committees were able to precipitate actions from which the Assembly and the City Corporation shrank; furthermore, mechanics had greater power in the committees because in extra-legal politics the forces of tradition and the law—customs of deference and laws disfranchising a few of the poorest—were less apparent and less rigidly observed. Once having made an entrance, it was relatively easy for the tradesmen to transfer their political presence from the extra-legal to the legal sphere. In 1776, however, the radical program began going beyond the traditional political objectives of tradesmen. The extreme radicals—including some mechanics, but not representing either the interests of or the traditional program or the weight of the artisan community—began championing the cause of new men entering politics who came from more meager circumstances than those who had participated in urban political affairs heretofore, and for whom it was imperative not only to enter politics through the extra-legal door, but also to have a change in the election laws which excluded them from voting privileges. For example, extreme radicals were less successful in a special election of May 1776 to fill newly created Assembly seats in the city than they had been in a recent extra-legal election, probably because election rules were more strictly enforced than in extra-legal elections. Philadelphians followed their normal election procedures and rules in extra-legal elections, but in times of patriotic fervor it was probably difficult to exclude the zealous, especially since the only teeth behind the franchise restriction was the threat of public exposure—a threat not likely to be carried out by the dominant radicals.[39] Thus, for the first time in 1776, the question of francise exclusion in regular (legal) elections became important to radicals.

In April of 1776, just before the special May election for new assemblymen, "An Elector" complained that the franchise laws discriminated against those of modest circumstances in the city.[40] "Civis," representing the voice of tradition, replied, and charged "An Elector" with designing to open the polls to "minors and apprentices, . . . [and] new men lately arrived among us. . . . Such men, if they are permitted to vote, will be easily influenced to vote for that party who raise them to consequence by giving them the rights of citizens before the law and constitution of the province."[41]

"Civis" exaggerated when he asserted that those demanding enfranchisement were "minors and apprentices;" the kind of citizen "An Elector" championed was the man who had already served an apprenticeship and had "set up to be a housekeeper for himself"— that is, the ordinary common man, who had experienced difficulties qualifying for the franchise. At the last election (the special election of May 1776), many men were challenged at the polls, he explained, and thus voting became "troublesome, partial and precarious, giving advantage to the *profligate* and *corrupt,* and putting it in the power of introverted persons to tire and affront the most worthy men so as to avoid taking their votes."[42] Thomas Paine's maxim that voting rights could be established by ownership of almost anything a man "could call or even think his own" was being challenged in 1776, in a last-ditch effort by traditional political forces to stem the ineluctably rising radical tide.[43]

Notwithstanding radical complaints about franchise restrictions, the Assembly made no move to modify the law. But modification became unnecessary, for two weeks later the Continental Congress adopted its famous resolution that Americans ought to form new governments "where no government sufficient to the exigencies of their affairs" existed, and this was all the excuse radicals needed to seize power.[44] A radical caucus within the Philadelphia Committee called a meeting of the inhabitants at which they pushed through a resolution favoring a provincial convention to form a new state government.[45] After an intensive progaganda campaign by the radical Philadelphia Committee and the Committee of Privates, a provincial conference of committees met to lay the ground rules for a constitutional convention.[46] Seven of Philadelphia's tradesmen attended the conference of committees as part of the city's delegation, only two of whom had been active in politics before 1774.[47] Again, radical politics had moved far beyond both the original mechanic program and leadership of 1770–74, and even beyond the general concepts which underpinned the moving radical program and leadership in which mechanics participated during 1774–76.

Since the question of the franchise had recently become a matter of importance to Philadelphia's radical party, it was natural that the triumphant revolutionaries should urge the provincial conference to tamper with it in order to assure voting privileges for the lower elements of the city, where part of their urban support lay. The conference expanded the franchise to include all who had reached the age of twenty-one, who were military associators, who had resided in Pennsylvania for one year, and who had paid taxes in any amount; the only restriction on the franchise was an exclusion of those who refused to attest their loyalty to a new government founded "on the authority of the people only."[48]

Having already stacked the deck of the Constitutional Convention election, the radical leaders of Philadelphia—Paine, Matlack, Young, and Cannon—undertook an extensive propaganda campaign in which citizens were urged "to chuse no rich men, and few learned men as possible to represent them in the Convention."[49] Pennsylvanians did as they were bid, and the preponderance of the new state's constitutional delegates were "men of small property and learning," and without experience in public affairs—or, as one uncharitable lady said, the convention was filled with "numsculs."[50]

Carefully guided by the radical leaders from Philadelphia, the Constitutional Convention sponsored one of the most democratic state constitutions to appear in America during 1776. It guaranteed freedom of religion, free elections, security of property, freedom of speech, press, assembly, and petition, and the right to bear arms; it stated the people's rights to regulate internal policy, to make their governmental officers accountable, to recall officers, and to be free from peacetime standing armies. Far more important, it provided for a unicameral legislature, vested with predominant political power. The executive could neither originate nor veto legislation, and the judiciary lost its permanent tenure. Even the legislature was severely limited by the democratic voice of the people, however: it was annually elected, and no legislator was allowed to serve more than four years in seven; the body was required to publish its proceedings before enacting laws, and it was required to keep its doors open to the public.[51] Anything but a Jeffersonian government, the new Constitution of 1776 gave enormous political influence to the electing constituency.

The only thing which was *not* democratic about the Constitution of 1776—and this irked its opponents as much as its egalitarian features—was the way in which it was adopted. The authors of the instrument, fearful it would not meet immediate popular consent, railroaded it through the convention.[52]

The radical victory in 1776 was so stunning and extreme that it was bound to produce a reaction, especially in Philadelphia, where moderate and conservative merchants had traditionally enjoyed predominant influence in politics. The Constitution of 1776 coalesced new political parties, one of which provided a voice for men of moderate political views in Philadelphia. The so-called anti-constitutionalists hoped they could prevent the Constitution from becoming operative by winning enough seats in the legislature to scuttle the ship before it could sail.[53] Some mechanics may have backed the radical (or Constitutionalist) party, though it is possible only to guess about their voting behavior. The radical ticket included several tradesmen who had risen to power since 1774, and contemporary observers believed citizens of modest means were more radical than "the Respectable Citizens of Fortune and Character."[54] Alexander Graydon observed that "as Whiggism declined among the higher classes, it increased in the inferior; because they who comprised them, thereby, obtained power and consequence."[55]

Yet although some of the "meaner" mechanics may have voted for the radicals, the majority of the community probably did not. For the radical ticket lost by a two-to-one margin in Philadelphia, an event that would not have occurred had mechanics voted as a body for the radicals.[56] Although the moderate anti-constitutionalists won in Philadelphia, however, they lost in frontier counties, where the real radical voter strength lay, and the first leigislature under the Constitution of 1776 was therefore seated with a slim radical majority. Not willing to take defeat graciously, the anti-constitutionalists boycotted the Assembly to prevent a quorum, and as General Howe's triumphant army marched across New Jersey effective government came to a grinding halt in Pennsylvania.

Discouraged and demoralized, Philadelphians seemed on the brink of giving up the Revolution during December of 1776.[57] Only after Washington's signal victory at Trenton did Pennsylvania spirits rally, and there developed in midwinter of 1776–77 a consensus to live with the Constitution of 1776 at least until the war crisis abated.[58] By spring of 1777, moderates were declaring "their entire concurrence in and support of every measure for the public defense; that they would suspend their proceedings respecting forms of government, and would be wholly ruled by the sense of the majority of the State, be it either to alter the present one or confirm it."[59] Whatever the quality of the Constitution of 1776, it would have a "fair experiment" before it was finally judged.[60]

The success of the Revolution in Pennsylvania hung in balance during the year following Independence, because political parties were identified with fundamental philosophical positions. Questions of principle obscured the operational or practical aspects of government. Yet it would be in the day-to-day successes and failures of government that the strength of the Revolution was tested, as much as in the grander battles of principle. We have only a few brief glimpses of municipal government in this period, but these few reveal orderly behavior. The street commissioners, wardens, and city commissioners (who replaced the tax assessors and collectors) resumed and expanded their administration of government when the moribund Corporation disintegrated. Mechanics continued to figure prominently in these offices, as they had prior to 1776: at least seven of the ten elected officials in 1776–77 were artisans. In addition, mechanics held one-third of the seats in the municipal judiciary in 1776, increasing this share to one-half in 1777.[61] Quietly, and without fanfare, the common man of Philadelphia had accomplished one of the great objectives of the Revolutionary movement—placing the power of government wholly in the hands of those who were governed.

The Fortunes of War, 1776-83

THE first two years of independence in Philadelphia were dis-
jointed and chaotic. Since the Constitution of 1776 departed substantially from the political traditions of Pennsylvania, it naturally
evoked powerful forces of opposition which divided the people.[1]
Moreover, the military activities in the vicinity of the city created
uncertainties which affected politics. Philadelphia's occupation in
1777 suspended, without resolving, the tangled political process
brought on by Independence, and thus it was not until 1778 that the
bizarre and confusing began to be supplanted by a more normal
process of political development. As the occupation army left, and
the war shifted to distant fronts, Philadelphians returned to the
business of making their revolutionary settlement free from outside
pressures.

The war continued to exert some influence on Philadelphia, of
course. The manufacturing sector of the economy, for example,
worked at peak productivity. Not only did the war effectively screen
out all competing English wares, but demands of the American military effort stimulated the expansion of several manufacturing enterprises, particularly ship-building, textiles, and weapons-making.[2] In
some cases demand was so strong that it may have temporarily altered the traditional organization patterns of the city. Several of the
new enterprises were factories employing women, the poor, military

prisoners, and sometimes established craftsmen (though the latter more often were related to the factories as sub-contracting entrepreneurs, rather than as wage-earners[3]). Thus the war eliminated one of the most persistent economic problems of artisans by creating an expanding market on which they did not have to compete with cheaper imported goods. At the same time, however, other economic problems arose which caused manufacturers great hardship and which encouraged them to enter the political fray with force and determination.

A major crisis was produced by America's system of war finance. During the first year of hostilities, Congress had met expenditures by the traditional mode of currency finance; that is, it had emitted paper currency, without specie backing, promising to retire it at a future date by making it acceptable for tax payments.[4] Under ordinary circumstances, the paper currency might have maintained its credit and assisted the growth of trade and manufacturing as it had in the past; but the extent of the war effort was enormous, and in order to pay for Continental military operations, Congress was obliged to continue emissions of paper (by 1779 it had made over forty) in excess of what even a booming war economy could absorb. Furthermore, the states, which were also hard pressed for money, used the currency they acquired (since Congress itself had no power to tax, the Continental bills were accepted for tax payments by the states) to meet expenditures, rather than retiring it for the national government. As a result, excessive amounts of paper money flooded the market and caused a natural depreciation.[5] In Pennsylvania, the national currency problem was aggravated by a similar over-issuance of state government currency.[6] The year 1779 was critical: in the space of twelve months, currency depreciated from one-half its face value to one-sixtieth, and the downward plunge showed no signs of abating.[7] For Philadelphia artisans the situation became tragically ironic: the demands placed on their manufacturing capacities were great, yet their incomes melted in their hands.

The government's strategy for coping with the economic emergency had two essential characteristics. The dominant radical party believed it could attack the cause of depreciation—currency plethora—by governing its effects—inflated prices; and it attempted to use crude political arguments to bolster its control program (and perhaps, too, to obscure the shortcomings of the policy[8]). To get control of the mushrooming inflation, radicals proposed a price-freeze and a gradual rollback of prices.[9] A similar program attempted by the Assembly earlier in the spring had failed, in the radicals' view, because the methods used to implement it were faulty.[10] The crisis was one of extreme proportions, and as such, the radical mind reasoned, it was not subject to the normal forces of government: "there are offenses against society which are not in all cases offenses against law, and for which no written laws can be timely construed, or sufficiently applied."[11] At the root of the unfolding economic calamity, radicals testified, was a cadre of "engrossers" and "forestallers" who conspired to inflate prices artificially by withholding large quantities of goods from the market.[12] The Assembly's earlier program had failed because it had used traditional governmental means to attack the problem.

Having defined the problem as a social crisis, rather than as a matter of economic policy, it was natural for radicals to draw upon their experience in a former crisis, and to employ an extra-legal committee to carry out a control program, rather than rely on the government.[13] The manufacturing community at first supported this program and participated in its articulation and implementation.[14] By midsummer there were some indications that the price freeze was working, and the city committee sought to broaden its constituent base by a membership expansion. An election was held at which 120 citizens were appointed to a new committee, at least half of whom were mechanics.[15]

The success of the radicals' price freeze was short lived, however. Toward the end of the summer, prices began to soar once again, despite the committee's attempts to stem the tide. Ironically, one of the most telling blows against the control system came from the artisan group which had greatest representation on the extra-legal committee—the cordwainers and other leather craftsmen. They complained in midsummer that their wares were closely regulated, "while those of other tradesmen . . . are permitted to remain unregulated"; that the ceilings in leather crafts were disproportionately stiff; and that raw materials had been purchased at an advanced price (before regulation), while the goods wrought from those materials had to be sold at lower, regulated prices. "In fine," the leather craftsmen concluded,

> what tradesman will purchase raw materials and exert his industry and expend his money, in converting them into useful wares, when he knows that before they are fit for sale, they will be depreciated in his hands below the first cost of his materials? It is absurd and contrary to every principle of trade, . . . it will destroy every spring of industry, and will make it the interest of everyone to decline all business.[16]

The leather craftsmen had a point: to regulate prices was to treat the symptoms, not the cause, of the economic disease. The city's ailing economy required comprehensive and fundamental reorientation, not a superficial treatment like a price freeze.

A cleft was forming in the manufacturing community and among Philadelphians generally. "A Whig Shoemaker" claimed that "four fifths of the master workmen concerned [with the leather craftsmen's petition] . . . are persons disaffected to the common cause," while the petitioners contended that "The grand objective of the City Committee, we apprehend, should be to appreciate the current money, and not what they have mistaken for the same thing to regulate prices."[17]

Although the expanded price-freeze committee chosen on August 2 was elected by a very substantial majority, its support among Philadelphians appears to have been based more on the vehemence of its stance than on genuine public confidence.[18] At a pre-election public meeting, Republicans who wished to speak against the radicals' schemes were shouted into silence by a militant band of club-swinging thugs.[19]

The amount of violence in the streets of Philadelphia is a barometer of the people's frustration during the summer of 1779. As early as May, the economic crisis had produced "Threatening Handbills" and fear of mob violence.[20] A few days before the election of the first price regulation committee, one gentle lady reported "Men with clubs, have been to several stores, obliging the people to lower their prices," and for several weeks thereafter small bands of vigilantes roved about the streets threatening and occasionally arresting fellow citizens, claiming to act on authority of "the Populace."[21] Ever since Philadelphia had returned to American hands in 1778, there had been a strong undercurrent of resentment against suspected tories and Quakers—"the disaffected, Inimical, or self Interested" as one memorial described them—who had remained in town during the British occupation and who now appeared to be foremost among the monopolizers and forestallers.[22]

Surviving historical records do not reveal much about the violence and vigilantism in Philadelphia's streets during the difficult summer of 1779, but we do know it had class overtones in which mechanics figured largely. For example, "A Citizen of Philadelphia" asserted that "the poor laboring man, the mechanics, or the poor widows and families that are out of business" were the chief victims of the "avaricious disposition" of designing merchants and tories.[23] The leadership of the price-freeze committee, as well as of a special committee which in May had promised to ferret out tories, were from the lower and middling classes; the tactics and rhetoric condoned or encouraged by the leadership were the tactics and rhetoric of the rougher elements in society; the complaints which motivated action in the streets were the complaints of people of small circumstances.[24] We can also say with some certainty that Philadelphia's politics was running an uncontrolled course during mid-1779. As Benjamin Rush put it, public policy was breathing "the spirit of town meetings and porter shops."[25] According to three observers, roving bands of self-appointed policemen had as much control over the use of local jails as the legally constituted government.[26]

As the economic crisis deepened and as successive attempts failed adequately to cope with it, political power rapidly diffused into the streets.[27] The enlarged price-freeze committee which had been swept into office on August 2 with a clear and powerful mandate began to lose its unanimity by early September, and one exasperated radical condemned its members as "too numerous to execute with dispatch and too various in their ideas to concur in all the measures expected of them."[28] As the committee divided against itself, the center of radical gravity began to shift away from it and into the city's militia organizations. Since before Independence, militia companies had acted as forums for political discussion and springboards for political action, and they had been active in support of the committee's price-regulation schemes earlier in the summer; but now, led by a revived Committee of Privates, they began to succeed the committee itself as the root of power.[29]

The famous "Fort Wilson Riot" of October 4, is indicative of the disheveled state of Philadelphia politics at this time. By the end of September, price regulation had become a manifest failure as public policy, and the economy was once again rocketing toward complete disintegration; the August 2 committee gave up and passed out of existence late in September, which meant that the only remaining active organizations with distinctly radical political sentiments were the militia companies.[30] Without really knowing what they were going to do, or how, the common people turned to their militia companies for a solution to their "gloomyness" and "perplexities."[31] On October 4, the Committee of Privates ordered the militia to meet on the Common near Byrne's Tavern "on business of importance."[32] At Byrne's, the men entered some resolutions and it was suggested that they might settle the city's score with certain "persons suspected of disaffection."[33] The militia men then marched about town passing at one point the home of James Wilson, a moderate jurist and politician of wealth and power, where a number of the supposed disaffected had gathered, determined to defend themselves collectively from the mob.[34] Surviving accounts differ as to who started the shooting, why shooting began at all, and how many were shot, but several men of the mob were killed and wounded, and many more were clapped in jail by a corps of lighthorsemen under the command of the President of Pennsylvania.[35] The next day violence very nearly erupted again when some militia men contemplated forceably freeing their comrades; it was prevented by the timely release of the men on bail and by the conspicuous absence from the city of some of the Fort Wilson defenders.[36]

The so-called "Fort Wilson Riot" had a cathartic affect on Philadelphia. It cleansed the air of violence which had been building in tempo since early spring, for both parties to the affair of October

4 appear to have been thoroughly frightened by what had occurred.[37] It also had the affect of artificially hardening political loyalties temporarily in the city: although the radical economic program, including its powerful anti-tory invective, had proved inadequate to the task of rescuing the sinking economy, and although the radicals had been repudiated by many merchants, some mechanics (the cordwainers), and even by some members of the August 2 committee itself, nonetheless, radical politicians won a stunning victory in the fall Assembly election of 1779.[38] Insofar as the common folk, including mechanics, were responsible for returning a radical slate in Philadelphia, they were probably motivated primarily by emotion. It was only two weeks since Fort Wilson, and only three since the radical committee had abdicated; rational political opinion undoubtedly had not caught up with the blinding pace of events. Since before the Declaration of Independence, radicals had usually been able to count on mechanics for political support. The Patriotic Society—a prewar mechanics' organization—had been revived in 1778, and actively supported radical political candidates, now known as Constitutionalists.[39] The Constitutionalists liked to claim that "the opposition to the Constitution arose, and was supported only by a junto of gentlemen in Philadelphia who wished to trample upon the farmers and mechanics, to establish a wicked Aristocracy."[40]

Notwithstanding this strong traditional connection between mechanics and agrarian radicals, the bond began to erode after the autumn of 1779. The reason for the erosion was that the original alliance of rural and urban constituencies in the radical party was based on weak and transitory political concerns. The conjunction of "farmers and mechanics" in radical propaganda was a rhetorical flourish used to express egalitarian sentiments; they liked to argue that men on the lower end of the social ladder—mechanics and other laborers in the city, and yeomen on the frontier—deserved more power in determining public policy. It is true that the urban poor (which included many who were not mechanics) shared a common bond with farmers in that both had been outside of the Colonial political system somewhat, but once the immediate issues of political participation had been resolved (in part by the provisions of the 1776 Constitution, and in part by the decline of political deference in the early 1770s), the remaining common denominators between farmers and artisans were few and inconsequential. Moreover, the opposition party gradually abandoned its attacks on the 1776 Constitution, thus removing the external threat which helped hold the farmer-artisan alliance together. Anti-constitutionalists, who became known as Republicans, began to claim instead that they could run the poorly constructed political machinery better than the radicals.[41]

The electoral behavior of Pennsylvanians generally also had an affect on the attachment of mechanics to the Constitutionalist party. In 1778, Constitutionalists had lost the Assembly election in the city by a narrow margin, while their victory elsewhere in the state had been very substantial. This lopsided victory in rural constituencies caused the party to look to the west, not the city, for both leadership and guidance in the formation of party platform.[42] There were many matters on which rural yeomen and city mechanics were developing different views, and when the choice had to be made, the Constitutionalist party tended to throw its lot with the agrarian common man, not the urban.

The most important such matter was the economy. Philadelphia mechanics desperately needed a resolution of the deepening crisis which had precipitated so much violence in the city during 1779. At first they backed the radicals (the urban wing of the Constitutionalist party), but it gradually became apparent that their program was not meeting the needs of Philadelphia's commercial economy. As the cordwainers had pointed out, the radical program was a simplistic solution to a complex problem—an inadequate local antidote to a national economic malady.[43] An indicator of the failure to meet the needs of urban businessmen is that radicals had to rely on invective political rhetoric, and ultimately on violence, rather than on the persuasiveness of the success of their economic policy itself.

Recognizing the crumbling of the Constitutionalists' hold on mechanics, Republicans began actively to pursue artisan votes in 1779 and 1780. A recent change in apportionment of representation had boosted Republican Assembly strength, and the party realized that if it could win the seats allocated to Philadelphia it might obtain a thin legislative majority in 1780.[44] Appealing to mechanics' pocket books, Republicans contended that Philadelphia's economic problems could be solved in conjunction with a reformed national economic policy. In the face of this new offer of economic salvation, the old radical rhetoric quickly lost its appeal among mechanics and among Philadelphians generally. By election day, 1780, popular sentiment had been so far moved that Republicans won by a handy three-to-one majority—a majority they could not possibly have obtained without the support of mechanics.[45] Commanding a majority in the state legislature for the first time, Republicans inaugurated a program closely tied to national economic policy which restored health to the Philadelphia economy.

The history of the years 1779 and 1780 reveals once again the moderate character of Revolutionary sentiment among Philadelphia mechanics. Artisans were in the vanguard of extreme radical politics in 1779, just as they had been in 1770 and 1774; insofar as they participated in, and gave leadership to, the violent mob activity of the summer of 1779, they came about as close as they ever came to bringing about genuine class-related Jacobin "convulsion" among the people of Philadelphia.[46] But the events of 1779 stopped short of the wholesale social upheaveal they seemed to portend: Fort Wilson turned out to be a terminal, not an inaugural, event in the city's tortured wartime history.[47] Philadelphians stepped back from the ultimate Revolutionary brink and sought solutions to their problems in policies designed to advance the commercial business interests which were the common denominator of most urban citizens, mechanics as well as merchants.

Republican economic policy was simple and direct. Contending that the economy would right itself automatically if it were freed of artificial restraints, Republicans refused to consider any trade regulations except the "5 percent plan," an *ad valorem* tariff which would give Congress a tax income. To end currency problems, the Republican Assembly, urged on by Robert Morris, repealed tender laws and allowed paper money to depreciate until it passed out of circulation entirely. Having written off the past—the plan was a direct repudiation of just debts—Republicans tried to prevent future fiscal disasters by putting the economy on a specie basis, so far as possible.[48] They created the Bank of North-America, which financed government war purchases through short-term specie-backed loans and which aided the expansion of commercial business (both mercantile and manufacturing) in the same manner.[49]

During the remainder of the war, the Republican economic program revived mechanic and merchant fortunes, as its sponsors had predicted it would. The stability of the bank's notes, which became a currency, was assured by the institution's reputation, its connection with the government (which was the principal stockholder) and its conservative financing. Moreover, the credit provided by the Bank of North-America, although it was designed primarily for merchants, was put to good use by many artisans in the city. With military operations in another part of the country, with demand for manufactured wares still high, and with a stable and growing economy, artisans enjoyed unprecedented prosperity from 1781 to 1783. Sometime later, a mechanic reminisced wistfully about the last three years of the war: the Bank of North-America, he said, had adequately provided the credit necessary for the expansion of artisan industries: "Houses and ships were built, and improvements in manufactures of all kinds were carried on by money borrowed occasionally at the bank. Commerce and [mechanical] arts fluorished in Philadelphia, while they declined in every other city in America, from the want of that credit which the bank produced in our city."[50]

Because their economic policies effected a return of commercial prosperity, Republicans enjoyed the support of all urban constituencies, including the manufacturing community, virtually unchallenged in 1780, 1781, and 1782, and the party was able to control an Assembly majority throughout these years.[51] There remained a submerged counter-tendency in the artisan community—which was the remnant of the 1777–79 radical coalition. Characteristically, it put high premium on political ideology, rather than economic policy.[52] At no time during the remainder of the war did this residual radical sentiment seriously color the city's politics, yet its survival in this period, even though in minimum form, provides an important link between the years which preceded and followed the era of Republican supremacy. The printer Francis Bailey was the leader of this interest among tradesmen, and his newspaper, the *Freeman's Journal*, became the principal Constitutionalist propaganda implement in Philadelphia. At first, Bailey had difficulty finding an audience, but after 1782, an increasing volume of artisan opinion found its way into his columns. Constitutionalists were preparing the ground for the postwar period, in which they would make one final attempt to seal a bond between agrarian and manufacturing interests. The appearance of the *Freeman's Journal* in Philadelphia did not go unnoticed in the circle of mechanics who were committed to the Republican economic program: exactly a year later, Eleazer Oswald began publication of the *Independent Gazetteer*, which was designed as an antidote to Bailey's paper. The ebullient Oswald was an ideal publisher for such a journal, for he was an avid democrat and intensely tenacious of his rights, yet he was also consistently loyal to commercial economic principles.[53] He was a formidable opponent, because Constitutionalists were unable to use their standard rhetoric against him: a man with so much of the John Wilkes in him was not an easy target for the party of radical democrats.[54]

During most of the period from 1780 to 1783, Republicans neither had, nor required, a newspaper mouthpiece, for consensus among all Philadelphians was firmly enough rooted to make argumentation all but unnecessary. Yet the polemics of Francis Bailey and the Constitutionalists were not entirely in vain. As soon as the war ended, artisans were once again thrown into an adverse economic situation which gave radicals all the material they required to capitalize on the claims they had been making and to effect their first political challenge since 1779. The source of mechanics' trouble in 1783 was the very laissez-faire economic program which had worked so well theretofore. The most pressing postwar problem was the lack of restriction on international commerce, which permitted the same ruinous competition from British manufactories that had plagued tradesmen before the war. While war artificially restricted Philadelphia's greatest manufacturing rival, a free economy was considered desirable by artisans; but in time of peace it became an albatross.[55]

Philadelphia merchants could not complain that the war years had been economically spare. Indeed, many a sizable mercantile fortune was made as a result of the conflict.[56] Yet their past prosperity did not make them willing to let peacetime profits pass out of their hands in a protected economy. British warehouses were stocked full with goods for the American market, and Philadelphia merchants were anxious to obtain their share of the revived carrying trade. For this reason, they favored a continuation of the free-trade principles adopted in 1780. Thus Philadelphia's commerce re-opened without restriction in 1783, an event which was bound to provoke and annoy tradesmen.[57]

Soon after the port was opened, mechanics met to discuss the problem.[58] They complained of the "ruinous situation of their affairs, as well as . . . the fatal consequences which threaten their country, from the vast influx of foreign manufactures interfering with their particular branches of trade."[59] The chairman of the meeting, Robert Porter, conceded that mechanics had a private interest in commercial regulation, but emphasized the broader virtues of protection: "Nor will the mercantile interests of America escape the general calamity—These are also materially affected. —There is no merchant . . . that will not acknowledge the justice of [the mechanics'] cause, and espouse it."[60]

The tradesmen appointed a broadly representative committee to draft and present a petition to the legislature stating their case, and for the remainder of the year they persevered in the campaign. Nearly all the mechanics' argumentation was an attempt to work out an agreeable *modus operandi* between themselves and the merchant community in commercial terms.[61] For the most part, however, it fell on deaf ears, and as a result of the rebuff, opinion within the manufacturing community began to regroup and to gravitate toward the Constitutionalist party.[62]

Francis Bailey, who had long searched for a basis on which to revitalize the old farmer-artisan connection, eagerly exploited this rift between merchants and mechanics. Constitutionalists did not at first offer much to mechanics on the subject of the tariff, but relied instead on the rancorous, class-related rhetoric, liberally basted with tory-baiting, on which they had built a coalition of urban and rural common men in the period before 1779. There was, Constitutionalists alleged, a conspiracy afoot whose purpose it was to wipe out the democratic achievements of the Revolution.[63]

The Constitutionalists' initial campaign in the city drew some mechanics away from the Republican party, but it did not succeed in re-welding the old radical coalition.[64] The tariff was so important to tradesmen that no amount of political propaganda or xenophobia could convince them to support a party which would not directly pledge itself to secure the one measure which would save them from ruin.[65] Thus, with both parties opposed to the tariff, Philadelphia mechanics seemed to have no choice but to strike out on their own. On the eve of the 1783 election, "A Brother Mechanic" addressed the manufacturing community:

> It is said you are about uniting with what is called the Constitutionalists—but remember that if the republicans are unfriendly to your interests, the Constitutionalists are not more favorable or sincere. . . . Their views . . . extend not beyond their party interests—they wish to flatter and make you subservient to their purpose of getting into the offices of government; and when fixed in the saddle of state, like the Republicans, will consider you as a useless set of beings.[66]

He urged artisans to vote for a separate ticket in the election and if this should fail to produce the desired results he suggested the formation of a "Society of Mechanics" to further the cause.

Artisans followed the advice of "A Brother Mechanic" and drew up an independent ticket for the annual election.[67] The outcome of the election was not satisfactory, however: drawing on the residual strength of their success during the past three years, Republicans won the city election—a victory which allowed them to keep a bare majority in the legislature.[68]

For mechanics, the election of 1783 was a political disaster. Before 1783, they had always swung a lot of weight in city politics by acting as a balancing force between two closely contending parties, each of which was seeking to build strength by linking the manufacturing community to other constituencies. By withdrawing from the two-party battle in 1783, they not only failed to win legislative seats for their own candidates but they also lost their ability to influence those who *did* win by being part of a victorious or contending coalition. It was unrealistic of mechanics to strike out on their own in 1783, for they had neither the numerical strength nor the political experience to succeed. The fact that they did isolate themselves politically is testimony to the depth of their commitment to the tariff. Knowledgeable and familiar with the political system, they probably understood the consequences of separating themselves from both parties, and yet the acuteness of their economic distress (especially when compared with the prosperity of the period from 1780 until 1783) was so great that compromise was unacceptable, no matter what the political consequence, and no matter how attractive its other consequences. For the first time since 1770, the politics of the manufacturing community became distinctly focused and isolated. And—as in 1770—so long as it remained bereft of connections to or alliances with other factions, it was unable to affect significantly the body politic.

§❦§❦§❦§❦§❦§❦§❦❦§ VIII ❦❦❦❦❦❦❦❦❦❦❦❦❦❦

The Urban Coalescence, 1783-86

THE election of 1783 was a sobering experience for Pennsylvania's Constitutionalist party. With postwar economic and political adjustments in the immediate offing, everyone recognized that the party in power would exert enormous influence over the direction of the state for years to come.[1] Constitutionalists missed a chance to control the state legislature in 1783, but they came sufficiently close to victory that they were inspired to sustain a year-long effort to turn the tables in 1784.[2] Part of their program involved a serious courting of the city artisans, with the object of rebuilding the precarious alliance of urban and rural common men. One issue they settled upon as having high potential for bringing life to this cause in the period after 1783 was the Bank of North-America.

The agrarian grievance against Robert Morris' bank was not one which immediately appealed to Philadelphia's manufacturing community. Rural Pennsylvanians opposed the institution because it had succeeded in promoting a commercial economy centered in Philadelphia at the expense of the interests of country yoemen who were outside the Philadelphia orbit.[3] The specie drainage accompanying resumption of unrestricted importation caused a money shortage, but the bank's credit mitigated this problem only in Philadelphia and its immediate environs; moreover, the bank's loans (which were made in small notes and which therefore created money) were not available to those requiring long-term mortgages.[4] It feared the depreciation which often accompanied long-term bills of credit, as well as "the universal inattention to just debts" among farmers.[5] In addition, it worried that "tender laws" might allow repayment of mortgage loans in depreciated paper money.[6] The bank's unwillingness to extend agrarian credit made it a prime target for Constitutionalist attacks.[7]

Mechanics, for somewhat different reasons, also favored a revision of the bank-dominated domestic economy. As the post-war specie drainage began to deplete the supply of circulating medium in the city, as well as in outlying parts, artisans became increasingly anxious to curb the policies of the Bank of North-America which appeared to contribute to the monetary evaporation. Furthermore, the short-term bank credit was expensive; during the flush war-years, mechanics had been able to purchase it easily, but when military contracts disappeared and British competition penetrated the local market, business slumped and the bank's credit became more difficult to afford.[8] As one Philadelphian bitterly complained,

> Usurious interest, high premiums, speedy and punctual returns of money lent, are inconsistent with the spirit of improvement; especially in a new country. This country therefore seems to be growing backward in point of improvement. The mechanic labors under the double difficulty of the impracticability of obtaining money to carry on his business, and the profusion of foreign goods, which prevents the sale of such articles as he could furnish.[9]

Whereas backcountry Pennsylvanians outside the commercial sphere of Philadelphia required a revolution in the prevailing credit and monetary system, city mechanics needed only greater access to existing credit.[10] Craftsmen believed that solution of their problems lay not in destruction of the banking system, but in limitation of the monopoly which allowed the Bank to dictate high credit terms. "A Mechanic," for instance, testified: "I am not for destroying the Bank which has been found so useful—it is like fire and water, which though the best and most useful servants, are also the most dangerous of masters."[11] Ebenezer Hazard wrote that the bank was "prejudicial to the middling and poorer classes of people who wanted money on interest; for, as the bank yielded 9, 12, and even 16 per cent, none could be had at the legal rate, which is 6, and many were much distressed for want of money who could give good security, but could not afford to pay so great an interest."[12]

Given the considerable difference in the reasons for opposition to the Bank, it is doubtful whether yeomen and artisans would have found grounds for allying on the issue had not Republicans blundered in their effort to secure the future of the institution, which they regarded as the sheet anchor of the economy. Early in 1784 (while Republicans still controlled the Assembly), an attempt was made to create a second commercial bank in Pennsylvania, which appeared to promise relief to artisans because it would have broken the Bank of North-America's credit monopoly.[13] The form and objectives of the new bank were to be identical to the old, but presumably a competitive institution would drive interest rates down.[14] This would ease commercial credit availability in the city, but of course it would not affect the mortgage credit dearth, except insofar as monetary confidence and stability in the commercial sector might eventually put banks in a position to take greater risks in the mortgage market.[15]

Hoping to head off the threat to its monetary and credit control, the Bank of North-America offered to expand its own stock to include the new bank's subscribers, arguing that increased resources in one institution would accomplish many of the same objectives as a two-bank system.[16] The offer was made attractive and it was accepted.[17] This discrete maneuver by the Bank of North-America staved off destruction of the monopoly, but it was a pyrrhic victory: the pledge of an easing of credit terms notwithstanding, the Bank's facilities remained beyond the reach of most tradesmen, for the continuing specie drainage made it necessary for the bank to curtail its credit operations, regardless of its expanded resources, a phenomenon which coincided with an accelerating influx of foreign manufactures which so depressed local manufactures that mechanics were without the means to afford high interest rates.[18]

Mechanics became so angered by the apparent sell-out of the bankers that they were easily swept up by the Constitutionalists' notion to destroy the bank altogether and to establish a brand-new credit and monetary system. By convincing Philadelphia artisans that a vote for Constitutionalist candidates was a vote against usury, the radical party considerably strengthened its appeal in the city during 1784. From the mechanics' point of view, a more direct route to the source of their economic troubles would have been a tariff, for this would have increased their ability to afford credit by expanding sales, and at the same time credit would have become more available because specie, the foundation of bank credit, would have been conserved.[19] Yet obtaining a tariff was not a politically feasible goal in 1784, no matter how necessary or desirable it may have been for the artisans. Neither party would make commitments—Republicans, because mercantile elements were still profiting from the trade glut, Constitutionalists because agrarian elements opposed measures which would raise the prices of manufactured goods—and in this situation the mechanics' best hope appeared to be with the anti-bank party.[20]

In terms of what it had to offer mechanics economically, the Constitutionalist party in 1784 was merely the lesser of two evils, but it made up for this inadequacy to some extent with political rhetoric. Although zealous democratic arguments do not appear to have had a penetrating influence on artisan electoral behavior in 1783, there is evidence that they did the following year. The kind of sentiment which began to well up in the artisan community in 1784 is reminiscent of the economic crisis of 1779; bitterly frustrated, mechanics were susceptible to the argument advanced by Constitutionalists that a designing aristocracy, composed mainly of wealthy tories, lay at the heart of Philadelphia's troubles.[21] One, for example, asked "Whether the militia who now parade on the commons of Philadelphia are not generally mechanics?" and complained that tories, conscientious objectors, and the British themselves were being encouraged at the expense of America's "firmest friends."[22] Even the anti-bank propaganda was cast in this mold: "A Friend to Liberty" contended that the Bank's success in scuttling the proposed competitor bank might "embolden this dangerous combination to interpose again . . . and thus our state may be enslaved to the bank."[23] Suspicious Republican activities in the state legislature were the target of Constitutionalist propaganda. After failing to capture control of the Council of Censors (the body empowered by the Constitution to alter, amend, or abolish the instrument of government at seven-year intervals) in 1783, the Republican Assembly attempted to legislate two of its pet reforms.[24] The first was the incorporation of the city of Philadelphia and the second, the repeal of the test laws. Neither measure affected artisans *per se*, but both tended to bear out the Constitutionalists' claim that a powerful aristocracy was solidifying its control in the state. Tradesmen, most of whom were from the lower and middle social echelons, were always wary of undemocratic tendencies in their government and were easily swayed by the radical analysis of these activities. Republicans favored corporate organization of the city for reasons of governmental efficiency; but Constitutionalists held that corporations were publicly irresponsible, subject to the whims of an exclusive membership, and akin to an "aristocratick police."[25] Republicans favored repeal of the test laws because they disfranchised many "non-jurors" —mainly Quakers who had refused to participate in the war—who tended to be Republican in their political behavior; but to Constitutionalists, such a measure was nothing more than delivering up the benefits of the Revolution to America's enemies.[26]

Philadelphia's Constitutionalists formed a new political organization in 1784 for the purpose of cultivating tradesmen. Francis Bailey, publisher of the *Freeman's Journal*, who had been the agency for the hitherto meager ties between Constitutionalists and artisans, was the chairman of the new Mechanical Society, and he used his columns liberally to advance the cause.[27] The organization looked with contempt upon "the influence of the merchant, who prefers his own present interest to that of the community," and declared that "The interests of the land-holder [i.e., the farmer], of the mechanics, and of the manufacturer . . . form that great general interest of the state, on which its solid riches and strength must depend."[28]

Some artisans still argued that since neither party would support the tariff, neither should receive the votes of the manufacturing community.[29] But this argument does not appear to have made any headway in 1784. The Mechanical Society worked hard on behalf of Constitutionalists, and its efforts were successful. Constitutionalist candidates received a majority of votes cast of the urban electorate, a victory which complemented sweeping victories in rural constituencies and guaranteed a new majority in the legislature.[30]

The economic program on which the Assembly's new Constitutionalist majority embarked was heavily weighted toward the interests of the state's agrarian elements. The new credit and monetary system was to have four interrelated parts: first the public debt owned by Pennsylvanians was to be assumed and funded by the state, the avowed purpose being to establish the government's credit and the side affect being to satisfy another of the Constitutionalists' electoral proponents, the public creditors; second, with credit established, there would be a limited emission of paper currency, which was to have no specie backing, but which Constitutionalists believed would not depreciate in light of the confidence resulting from state assumption of Revolutionary debts; third, to bolster the Assembly's income further and to aid in the assumption program, a land office was to be opened, which would sell the public domain; and finally, a loan office would be established, which would loan money (state paper currency) at moderate interest on land mortgage.[31] The loan office was an overt rejection of banking finance, for whereas the bank had serviced the city's commercial community primarily, the loan office would accommodate "the distant freeholders . . . with money on easy terms and at a reasonable interest."[32] To assure the success of the new economic order, Constitutionalists destroyed the old by repealing the charter of the nefarious Bank of North-America, which they found not "compatible with public safety, and that equality which ought to prevail between individuals in a republic."[33] The bank had announced it would not accept paper currency issued by the government, and this provided the excuse for repealing its charter. In addition, Constitutionalists charged it with usury and favoritism, with refusing long-term credit, with discrimination against farmers and mechanics, and with being under foreign influence.[34]

Notwithstanding the fact that Constitutionalists had made overtures to mechanics in the fall election of 1784, the economic program which they enacted during 1785 had little in it which would be helpful to the urban manufacturing community. The single element in the program which dealt directly with mechanics was a tax exemption. Anticipating that the new currency emission would help pay interest on the assumed public debt, Constitutionalists believed heavy taxes would be unnecessary; the small tax which *was* necessary as a supplementary revenue measure was arranged so that it fell with greatest force on the eastern counties, and mechanics were entirely exempted from it.[35] Yet this was a superficial aid. It would lend relief from the tax, but it would do nothing to alter the economic situation which made taxes difficult to pay. Although mechanics had been discontent with the high interest rates which the bank's monopoly had permitted it to charge, the destruction of the banking system altogether brought them even more hardship. One Philadelphian complained that

> in no period of the late war did the citizens of Philadelphia experience so much distress, as they have felt since the last session of the Assembly. The attack upon the Bank, by stopping the circulation of cash, has involved thousands in difficulties. Several mechanical businesses have been suspended, and the tradesmen, who have large sums of money due to them, suffer from the want of market money.[36]

When a committee was formed in the city to petition the Assembly to suspend its charter repeal act, five of the eight members were mechanics, including three from the Mechanical Society's executive committee.[37] Even the artisans who had encouraged the farmer-mechanic alliance in the 1784 election became disenchanted with Constitutionalists' economic schemes. Eleazer Oswald contended that "The friends of paper money . . . may be reduced to the following classes—1st Debtors, 2nd Speculators, and 3rd brokers— while its enemies are all *honest* lawyers, doctors, parsons, merchants, mechanics, and farmers."[38]

From the mechanics' point of view, everything hung on the single question of a tariff. Without protection against free importation of cheaper foreign goods, no economic mechanism—a bank, paper money, a loan office, debt assumption, tax exemption—could provide the necessary relief. As the post-war economic crisis deepened in 1785, they became increasingly vociferous on the subject, claiming that until Pennsylvanians' "unhappy predilection for foreign frippery and gewgaws" was curbed by a tariff, the economy would continue to depress.[39] The burgesses claimed in December of 1784 that a committee was working on the tariff matter, but tradesmen were impatient for results and resented the implied delay.[40] One wrote hotly,

> The present members of assembly for the city and county of Philadelphia, were put into the assembly by the votes of Mechanics, and for the express purpose of imposing duties on certain foreign manufactures, to enable the mechanics to live by their arts, as well as to save specie in the country. A session of above two months is now over, and nothing has been done for us but referring our petition to a Committee, which had been done two years ago by former assemblies.[41]

The Constitutionalist assemblymen from Philadelphia were not insensitive to the needs of tradesmen, nor were they insincere in their desire to obtain a tariff for them; but the problem they faced as legislators was no different from that which confronted them as candidates: the economic basis of the farmer-mechanic coalition in the party was weak. It was difficult to convince the agrarian element that a tariff was important. Legislation of this kind would require difficult negotiation and time-consuming persuasion. The depth of urban Constitutionalists' problem is revealed in the comments of one of their rural compatriots, who said he opposed tariffs as impractical and inexpedient, and suggested instead that the manufacturing sector of the economy should be allowed to disintegrate: "We are sincerely sorry for the manufacturing Americans. We allow it to be a partial misfortune to those who are bro't up mechanics, instead of farmers, the pride and support of the land. But we hope the evil will cure itself, and that the necessary number of mechanics amongst us will, like water, find their level."[42] City Constitutionalists' alleged tariff promise during the election campaign of 1784 was written off as loose talk by "inconsiderate men" who acted "imprudently."[43]

Mechanics reacted vigorously to this shabby treatment. In

March of 1785, a large group of cordwainers—always at the forefront of the manufacturing community—declared that it was "a
duty we owe to our country and to ourselves, to stop, as much as in
us lies, the importation of boots and shoes of all kinds."[44] The cordwainers resolved not to buy or sell any imported wares, "nor mend,
or suffer any of the same to be mended by any in our employ."[45] A
separate meeting of journeymen cordwainers, following their masters' lead, resolved "not directly or indirectly [to] work for any man
who buys or sells any . . . imported manufactures, or suffers the
same to be mended."[46] The cordwainers' compact was meant as a
threat, and it worked. By emphatically demonstrating the mechanics'
commitment to the tariff, it probably provided the jolt necessary to
force reluctant Constitutionalists to modify their ideas. The Constitutionalists' Assembly majority was not so secure that the party
could afford to alienate tradesmen and thereby lose the next election
in Philadelphia. During the spring of 1785, a tariff bill appeared on
the house floor, the preamble of which stated that "good policy and
a regard for the well being of divers useful and industrious citizens,
who are employed as artizans and mechanicks, . . . demand of us
that moderate duties be laid on certain fabricks and manufactures
imported, which do most interfere with and which (if no relief be
given) will undermine and destroy the useful manufactories of the
like kind in this country."[47]

Mechanics responded quickly to the Constitutionalists' tariff
bill. The Mechanical Society's executive committee drew up a petition suggesting modifications and amendments and the various
craft-groups were encouraged to meet to consider particular problems. "Unless this is done without delay," one newspaper said (perhaps sardonically), "it cannot be expected that the House of Assembly will be able to adopt any efficacious system for the protection of
our trade. For it is a well known fact, that perhaps three-fourths of
the members consist of farmers and country gentlemen, who never
had any opportunity or desire to inform themselves of the fundamental principles of trade and commerce."[48]

The Constitutionalists' tariff was a beginning, and mechanics
worked hard to secure its passage, which finally took place on the
eve of the 1785 election.[49] But unfortunately for Constitutionalists

it was too little and too late. The tariff was a kind of after-thought appended to the Constitutionalists' economic program, designed not as a complement to the credit and monetary schemes, but as a stopgap solution to the problems of the annoyingly vocal manufacturing community.[50] Because the Constitutionalists did not think of the tariff as an integral part of the city's and the state's economic policies, they never appreciated the inadequacy of the tariff they enacted. While it contained some useful provisions, as a whole it could not meet Philadelphia's need because it bore no relation to national economic policy. So long as other cities had less stringent tariffs (or none at all), effective protective duties would force commercial traffic away from Philadelphia, thus continuing the economic depression even though local industry was protected.[51] Constitutionalists failed to understand this, undoubtedly because, as agrarian-minded men, they had little appreciation of the integral relationships between the manufacturing and trading sectors of the urban commercial economy. But as the Constitutionalists elaborated their economic program during mid-1785, such an appreciation *was* rooting itself in the Republican party.

Philadelphia's merchant community had been engaged in organized opposition to the Constitutionalists' economic program from the moment it had been elaborated.[52] For the most part, the economic assumptions behind merchant thinking were familiar: they preferred hard money to soft, they favored corporate banks to monetary and credit systems based on currency finance or land banks. But another economic premise, until 1785 present but muted, began to emerge as a guiding force of their argument. It was that the economic salvation of Philadelphia and Pennsylvania were immutably bound to the well-being of the *national* economy.[53] That premise was applied to an economic policy proposal—also hitherto present but muted—during 1785: Republicans, led by Philadelphia's merchant community, announced themselves in favor of a national tariff. Merchants had always recognized the value of a tariff as a commercial measure, but had not been able to muster much enthusiasm for it, so profitable was the postwar trade. By 1785, however, trade was "quite knocked up," because the local market was glutted with

English merchandise and because Philadelphia merchants had sent off all their specie to pay for the mass of imported dry goods.[54]

The beginning of Philadelphia merchants' renewed interest in tariffs can be dated to the formation of a Chamber of Commerce in late 1784, the purpose of which was to coordinate the business activities of the merchant community, including its interests "in many of our most capital manufactories."[55] By the spring of 1785, merchants were making direct overtures to the city's mechanics.[56] The artisans were at first suspicious, for they had been too often mistreated by other interest groups.[57] By the end of June, however, there can be no doubt that a merchant-mechanic alliance was taking firm hold in the city. The merchants' committee called a general meeting of inhabitants which reaffirmed resolutions earlier adopted by the merchants calling for "a full power in Congress, over the commerce of the United States," and for tariffs to protect and promote local manufacturing.[58] The artisan community was cautiously supportive, resolving its agreement with the merchants' position *"so far as the views of that memorial extend."*[59] The pact between the two principal economic groups in the city was sealed by the addition of seven mechanics—including some who were leaders in the Mechanical Society, a Constitutionalist organization—to the leadership committee which had called the public meeting.[60]

The alliance of merchants and mechanics which was forged in June of 1785 was supplemented by the establishment of "The Philadelphia Society for the Encouragement of Manufactures and useful Arts," an organization of thirty-six citizens, eleven of whom were mechanics.[61] The activities of these economic and political organizations which brought merchants and mechanics together reflect an emerging urban-commercial coalition.[62] Both the articulated and implicit concerns of these organizations were determined by their participants' urban residence and commercial economic activity. When politically welded together with the commercially oriented forces in the counties immediately adjacent to Philadelphia, they would create a force which would dominate Pennsylvania until the close of the Federalist era. In 1785, they were only forming, however, and there is evidence that some mechanics were hesitating.

The Mechanical Society, for example endorsed Constitutionalist candidates in the fall election of 1785, even though many of its prominent members had allied themselves with Republican forces earlier in the summer.[63]

Constitutionalists did not go down without a fight in Philadelphia. On the eve of the 1785 election, they enacted their tariff measure (it was probably on this basis that they received the support of the Mechanical Society), and they tried desperately to avoid other economic questions, concentrating mainly on loaded rhetoric. "Mirror," for example, billed Republican ideas as a desertion of *"The common people,* such as farmers, tradesmen, mechanicks, and *others of the lower kind."*[64] Republican banking forces were accused of discouraging mechanic business expansion (by keeping credit artificially tight) because they feared that the economic prosperity of the manufacturing community would be accompanied by a challenge to merchants' political leadership.[65]

When they went to the polls in 1785, artisans of Philadelphia were in a difficult position. The leadership group (the Mechanical Society) had declared itself for the Constitutionalist incumbents; Constitutionalists had only days before enacted a tariff—a bad tariff, because it was local, rather than national, but nevertheless a tariff; and Constitutionalists had spoken squarely to mechanics' traditional suspicion of the wealthy and powerful merchant class. And yet there were forces driving mechanics the other way: "A Philadelphia Mechanic" contended that Constitutionalists were "at a loss to supply the immediate and urgent necessities of the mercantile part of the community, whose welfare is too much interwoven with that of mechanics not to thrive and decay with theirs."[66]

We have no way of knowing exactly how mechanics cast their votes in 1785, but we do know that the election was "a violent contest," and that a good portion of the artisans disavowed the leadership of the Mechanical Society.[67] It is doubtful that the Republican ticket, which carried the day in the city, could have won without substantial backing in the manufacturing community.[68]

The Republicans' Philadelphia victory reflected the party's ability to identify and champion economic issues on which there was broad consensus among the principal classes in the city, merchants and mechanics. The political coalition was not sufficiently successful in enough other constituencies to gain a majority in the state legislature, however. As a result, the emerging Republican power was given a year to mature and galvanize, and the agrarian-oriented economy was permitted a year of trial before its creators would again face electoral challenge in 1786.

Concluding the Revolution, 1786-89

THE inadequacy of the agrarian economic program from the viewpoint of those within Philadelphia's commercial sphere became increasingly apparent during the course of the year 1786. As a result, the urban coalition of mechanics and merchants, which had formed in 1785, solidified and was strengthened by the expansion of Republican influence in the agricultural areas adjacent to, and commercially involved with, the city. Constitutionalists had been swept into office in 1784 when Republican laissez-faire economic principles had permitted indiscriminate importation of British goods, the results of which were to depress prices, to throw mechanics out of work, to cause an unremitting specie drainage, to tighten credit, to diminish available circulating medium, and generally to dampen the entire economy. So far as the commercial community in and around Philadelphia was concerned, however, the Constitutionalist cure turned out to be worse than the disease.

The Constitutionalists' tariff, enacted on the eve of the 1785 election (possibly as a last-ditch attempt to retrieve lost ground in the manufacturing community), was an utter failure. By early summer, Philadelphians were complaining loudly that the tariff law was having the opposite of its intended impact: wherever Pennsylvania applied a protective duty, New Jersey and Delaware laid a light one, or none at all, with the result that her neighbors were able to draw off what little trade Philadelphia had enjoyed in the days before the tariff.[1] Nor did local manufacturing revive as a result of tariff protection: Philadelphia's coasting trade was so extensive that policing the law was nearly impossible and smuggling became flagrant.[2] Clandestine trade directly injured both the honest merchants and the mechanics and it inhibited the general economic rehabilitation for which the tariff's architects had hoped.[3] Moreover, the law itself was badly written: for example, one of its provisions—a high impost on cordage to protect native rope walks—made Philadelphia shipbuilding uncompetitive, with the result that many scores of mechanics in trades allied to ship construction were unable to find employment.[4]

Constitutionalist monetary policy, too, was unsuccessful in the city. The government's attempt to establish its credit notwithstanding, the paper money depreciated—an economic malady which had not pertained in the troubled years 1783–85, before Constitutionalists initiated their reforms.[5] Merchants had to pay for imported goods in specie, so they refused to deal in paper currency; mechanics, who often tried to equalize their competitive position by accepting paper money, found it useless when they, in turn, dealt with merchants. Furthermore, the state paper money had caused tightening of commercial credit which exceeded even the shortage mechanics had complained of in 1783 and 1784. The loan office was no help because its credit was based on land mortgage; Constitutionalists had hoped a general easing of credit would accompany their economic program, but this did not occur.[6] As the currency depreciated, monied men hesitated to engage in commercial lending, fearing an arbitrary "tender law" would make loans repayable in currency worth considerably less than its face value.[7]

Constitutionalists were fully aware by 1786 that the failure of their economic program had cost them the support of the principal commercial elements in Philadelphia, including their erstwhile allies, the mechanics. Since the realignment of the artisans with the Republican party seemed impossible to stop, Constitutionalists made a transparent attempt to cancel the loss through a franchise fraud. The tax law which Constitutionalists passed in 1785 to supplement the state's income had exempted tradesmen, a provision designed to garner support in the manufacturing community for the proposed program. In 1786, the Constitutionalists used this exempting proviso for the opposite purpose—not to win mechanic votes, but to destroy them altogether. They passed a new law for regulating elections which declared that "no citizens but those who are *rated for and pay taxes,* shall have a right to vote at elections."[8] This would have prevented mechanics, who were tax exempt, from casting votes, and at the same time would have reduced the Assembly representation from the city by decreasing the size of the voting constituency.

The plot failed. Eleazer Oswald, printer of the paper most involved in the affairs of mechanics, exposed it a month before the election, and the embarrassed Assembly moved "to entitle the mechanics to vote at the ensuing election, notwithstanding a clause of the *funding bill,* precludes them from that privilege."[9] But the motion came too late. Mechanics already had positive economic reasons for favoring Republicans, and this political chicanery sealed their sentiments against Constitutionalists. In the pre-election campaign, tradesmen were warned against the encroachments of "an *indigent* and artful Aristocracy," and urged "to withdraw [their] confidence" from Constitutionalists.[10] One artisan denounced what had passed for "a *mechanic* ticket" at former elections; Constitutionalists, he told craftsmen, "may have *appeared,* in some few instances, to consult your interest [but] their primary view, has been their own emolument."[11] Because of the attempted franchise fraud, he said, "Every obligation which you may have *supposed* yourselves under to the *Constitutionalists* (as they term themselves) is dissolved."[12]

Republicans handily won the city of Philadelphia in the 1786 election, and more important they also won enough other seats to obtain a majority in the legislature.[13] Oswald's *Independent Gazetteer* blared the victory: "The late returns of Assemblymen," a correspondent wrote, "fully evinces that the Bank of North-America has recovered its popularity, and that paper money has lost its credit throughout the state."[14] The Constitutionalist Party experienced a rapid twilight after the 1786 election, and never again posed a serious threat to Republican leadership, nor did it attempt to resurrect its Revolutionary bonds with mechanics.[15] During the year 1787 there was but a single newspaper editorial discussing the commonalities of farmers and artisans: "until ninety-nine of an hundred of the citizens of America are farmers, artificers or manufacturers," it said, "we can never be rich or happy."[16]

The return of a Republican legislative majority in the fall of 1786 did not immediately solve the mechanics' problems, for the economic system introduced by Constitutionalists could not be quickly undone. The 1785 tariff continued to divert much of Pennsylvania's regular trade to other ports, and a general commercial lull remained in the city. The Republican program of vesting commercial regulatory power in the national government would take time to effect. Paper money, too, continued to plague Philadelphia. It had been issued in the standard currency finance mold (with provision for its retirement by future taxation), and there was little Republicans could do to shorten its life-span. This became a source of increasing distress for artisans, because speculators bought up available depreciated currency, hoping the government would become impatient with tax redemption and buy it at near face value; thus even the depreciated paper money was in short supply.[17] As the amount of circulating medium decreased, the re-chartered bank's cautious credit issues could not effectively supplement the scarcity.

Although there was no immediate economic rejuvenation after the 1786 election, Philadelphia artisans' Republican sympathies did not sour. In part this is because the Republican program hinged on an expansion of the national government, a process which everyone recognized would take time. In part, also, it is because mechanics had become sophisticated in their thinking about the economy: they recognized the fundamental causes of their difficulties and were willing to wait out the solutions. George Bryan later pointed out that "Our Navigation was almost wholly in the Hands of Foreigners and the Sale of Merchandize in the same hands. The numerous classes of Tradesmen who depend on Commerce and particularly those who depend on Navigation [i.e., overseas trade] were distressed."[18]

There was broad consensus among all sectors of the urban economy that nothing short of a national tariff would resolve this

distress. "The mechanics and sailors know this to be truth," expostu-
lated one Philadelphian.[19]

Similarly, on the subject of paper money, artisans recognized
that it was the after-effects of Constitutionalists' bad monetary
policy, not the inadequacy of Republicans', which was causing the
bad times. "Curio" observed that "The paper money of 1785, has
been the cause of more uneasiness and chagrin to the mechanics and
labouring people of Philadelphia . . . than almost any one act of
government since the revolution."[20] Another newspaper correspondent noted that the old paper money was "starving our honest
tradesmen."[21] The need for a stable currency, like the need for an
effective tariff, led the manufacturing community toward the Republican position that resolution of commercial problems ultimately
depended upon establishment of a strong national government.[22] By
the fall of 1787, particularly after the secret workings of the Constitutional Convention were revealed, the manufacturing community
had become "highly federal."[23]

If mechanics had any doubts about the wisdom of their commitment to Republicans, they were probably relieved by the stren-
uous activities of the merchant community on behalf of the proposed
national economic program. In 1785, a group of merchants and mechanics had founded an organization known as the Society for the
Encouragement of American Manufactures and useful Arts; in
1787, a clique of Republican merchants, who were less interested in
the Society's original program of collecting and disseminating information about manufacturing than they were in the political foundation of the state's economy, captured control of the society and
transformed it into a powerful tariff lobby.[24] The society claimed that

> when by the establishment of a general government clandestine im-
> portation of foreign articles shall be prevented, and that preference
> given throughout the United States to the manufactures of America,
> which the common interest demands; our established manufactures
> will resume their former vigor and others will be found to flourish
> which have hitherto been little known among us.[25]

Mechanics agreed: a powerful central government with the capacity
and the will to protect and promote commercial interests on a na-

tional scale had come to be viewed as quintessential to Philadelphia's future.[26]

The fundamental issues posed by the Constitution of 1787 were second in importance only to those raised in 1776, for the document suggested a Revolutionary settlement which would have deep and lasting impact on the kind of society America would have. Americans appear to have recognized the profundity of the decision they were making when they considered the new Constitution.[27] And yet in Philadelphia the political activity surrounding the ratification of the 1787 Constitution is in no way comparable to the complex and intense history of the years between 1774 and 1776. There was, to be sure, heated argumentation between Federalists and Antifederalists in the public prints, but the battle was largely rhetorical.[28] Public meetings were few; extra-legal organizations never played a part in the contest; new faces and new forces failed to appear in politics; no one attempted to capitalize on uncertainty to introduce unfamiliar or radical social or political demands. All this was true because by 1787 most of the Revolutionary dust had already settled and there was among Philadelphians a general consensus in favor of the economic, social, and political principles embodied in the new Constitution.[29] As one Philadelphian put it, "The people of Pennsylvania have been so often told of *an appeal to arms,* when power and office (not liberty) were in danger . . . that they now regard the threat [described by Antifederalists] no more than a scolding of the apple women in Market Street."[30]

George Bryan, an Antifederalist, wrote a careful class-by-class analysis of the support for, and opposition to, the Constitution which explains the bases on which Philadelphia mechanics reached their conclusions about the propriety of the proposed new instrument of government: "such as depend on Commerce and Navigation in favor—the others divided according to their formed Attachments to the Revolution & Constitution of Pennsylvania or their Prejudices against them.[31] Two forces were pulling on mechanics: on the one hand they were sentimentally and politically attached to the Revolution of 1776 and to the political body which had been born in the fire of that moment, the Constitutionalist (now Antifederalist) party; and on the other hand, they were drawn toward the

Republican (now Federalist) party by broad economic and social considerations. The latter had the greater magnetism.

Bryan did not suggest strict "determinist" economic motives for those who favored or opposed the Constitution. Pennsylvanians were moved by a variety of concerns, ranging from those of the civil officers, who were threatened in the public prints with reprisals if they failed to declare themselves for the Constitution, to the women, about whom Bryan commented, alas, "all admire Genl. W."[32] Even his remark that it was dependence on commerce and "navigation" which influenced many Philadelphia mechanics was not an assertion of narrow economic motivation, for Bryan understood "commerce" to mean a complex system of economic interests, social values, and political attitudes. It was an intuitive understanding, not an analytic position. For example, he understood that both geographic location and population density, as well as an individual's calling and property, had something to do with how he might feel about the 1787 Constitution: "The Counties nearest the Navigation were in favor of it generally, those more remote, in opposition. . . . The Farmers were perhaps more numerous in opposition than any other Sett of Men—Most Townsmen were for it."[33]

By 1787, most mechanics were fully aware that their survival as manufacturers was predicated upon a government which valued urban communities in general, and which was able to take the steps to promote their growth and prosperity. On two separate occasions —1779 and 1784—politicians who lacked an understanding of, and appreciation for, the necessities of urban life had so tangled the economy as to make life in Philadelphia almost insufferable. When mechanics voted for the 1787 Constitution, they were voting for a new society which would put a premium on commercial prosperity in America's urban centers—a prosperity which would inevitably be reflected in their specific work as manufacturers, as well as in their way of life generally.

Not *all* mechanics were advocates of the new Constitution. According to Bryan, some had "attachments" to the radical cause of former days, attachments which gave them an Antifederalist "prejudice."[34] These mechanics represented the last vestige of the old farmer-artisan alliance in the Constitutionalist party. Forged in

1775–76, it had reached its zenith in the early war years; it all but disappeared during the period of Republican triumph, from 1780 to 1783, then returned briefly at the height of the postwar slump, only to be snuffed out again in 1785. Characteristically, when it appeared in the battle over the Constitution of 1787, it centered quite specifically on a question of political democracy: the absence of a bill of rights in the new Constitution. Mechanics had always been sensitive about democratic questions; it was, after all, on an issue of political participation that they had joined the Revolutionary struggle during the decade before Independence, and it was this sensitivity that made them subject to the rancorous, sometimes class-conscious political rhetoric in times when Constitutionalists had campaigned hardest for mechanic votes. Given this background, it would be expected that the manufacturing community would be affected by the Antifederalist case against the 1787 Constitution.

It was ironic, but not unnatural, that Eleazer Oswald, printer of the newspaper which had championed artisans' commercial concerns and their connection with Republicans, should become the leader of the small minority of Antifederalists among mechanics. Notwithstanding his great concern for commercial life in Philadelphia, Oswald was preeminently a democrat, and the absence of a bill of rights therefore governed his opinions. Yet his views were probably not much different from those of "A Mechanic," whose correspondence was published in Oswald's paper: while he opposed the Constitution because it lacked specific democratic protections, he nonetheless favored a reorientation of the economy in commercial terms and a move to give the national government broad commercial power. He concluded, "I am one of that class of citizens who suffer as much by dullness of the times, and scarcity of cash, as most others perhaps; and I ardently pray that they may mend, with the necessary *federal* powers to regulate commerce and our other general concerns."[35]

Aside from the grievance over the bill of rights, there was probably little ground for difference between "A Mechanic" and the vast majority of Philadelphia's tradesmen, who believed the new Constitution would be "a noble mansion for the residence of American liberty."[36] "A Pennsylvanian," who claimed to be a mechanic, testified that nearly all Philadelphians were Federalists, and that the proof lay in the fact that Antifederalist printers had no support.[37] Bryan agreed: "Col. Oswald was almost the only printer who published in Opposition in Philadelphia and . . . he had been injured in Consequence."[38] There can be little question that opposition to the Constitution was insubstantial in the city. Antifederalists were few in number, and their case was built upon a narrow foundation —a much narrower foundation than that which supported Antifederalism in agrarian America. It was based on a particular grievance, not on a commitment to a future social and economic and political order contrary to the one inherent in the proposed Constitution.

The process of ratification in Pennsylvania was smoothly engineered. In the annual election of October 1787, Republicans increased their Assembly strength.[39] Soon after it sat, the new legislature voted to call a ratifying convention, and in the election which followed, Federalists won by large margins in a majority of the constituencies, including the city of Philadelphia.[40] Bryan reported "Very little Bustle was made and little or no Opposition" in Philadelphia.[41] In the convention itself, all Antifederalist attempts to delay proceedings were easily quashed, and a final vote on ratification was passed on December 12, 1787, only a few weeks after the convention had been organized.[42]

Following the action of the Pennsylvania ratifying convention, a celebration parade was held in Philadelphia which affords a further indication of the mechanics' sentiments about the Constitution of 1787. Practitioners of the various crafts organized and marched in separate bodies, carrying "flags, devices and machines." The slogan on the rope-makers' banner read, "may commerce flourish"; sail-makers declared, "may commerce flourish, and industry be rewarded"; weavers said, "may government protect us."[43] Philadelphia's artisans and craftsmen appear to have believed the new Constitution would establish a social and economic order which valued and promoted the urban and commercial concerns in which they were so intimately involved.

Ratification of the 1787 Constitution was considered by mechanics to be a logical and satisfying culmination of the Revolutionary movement, not a thermadorian reaction against the principles and achievements of 1776. The great cataclysm of 1776 had projected Philadelphia tradesmen to the center of the urban political stage, but it had not established the preeminence of the urban commercial community itself. The new Constitution, in the view of most mechanics, had the potential for doing this without undoing their past Revolutionary achievements. Ratification generated a new optimism in the manufacturing community which was reflected in the celebration parade. It was also reflected in mechanics' organized efforts to gather "all the information attainable respecting the present situation of the different manufactures of this state" so that they could present a powerful and intelligent tariff case to the new national government as soon as it met.[44] The Revolution had not only given mechanics the right to participate in public affairs, it had now also given them the sense that they could participate effectively in a governing process which was oriented toward their needs, goals, and aspirations.

The mechanics' satisfaction with these developments was reflected in an ebullient public optimism. Printers commented frequently about the bright future of manufacturing and praised the establishment of new factories or ingeneous manufacturing innovations.[45] The Society for the Encouragement of Manufactures and useful Arts reverted to an energetic program of sponsoring and rewarding manufacturing advancements.[46] The anticipated benevolent influence of the 1787 Constitution cheered Philadelphia's manufacturing citizens, but even more encouraging was the fact that business began to revive in 1788—even before the new government was inaugurated. Several circumstances conspired to unbridle the city's small businesses: first, a decline in the cost of living made it possible for artisans "to work on lower terms, and . . . live well . . . by prices, which a few years ago would not maintain them"; second, the introduction of several European machines and inventions of native craftsmen boosted production in a few key industries; and third, a rise in the emigration of skilled artisans to Philadelphia in 1788 helped establish some emerging trades.[47] Everyone sensed a business boom in the making, and they plunged ahead eagerly.[48] One Philadelphian predicted that Pennsylvania "may become a

Great-Britain, with respect to arts and manufactures."[49] The city's spirits were so high by the autumn of 1788 that its support for Federalist candidates in the first Congressional and Presidential election was overwhelming. George Clymer and Thomas Fitzsimmons were publicly recommended by mechanics for election to the House of Representatives because they were considered friends of manufactures and because they were deeply involved in "city and commercial" matters.[50] Both were easily elected.[51]

With the economy apparently on its way to realizing the fondest dreams of the urban business community, the only remaining unfinished business of the Revolution was the adjustment of the state's internal political system to the new realities of national politics. The process began somewhat before ratification of the Constitution, in 1786, when Republicans already had the majority necessary to work their will in the state. The test laws were repealed, and the city of Philadelphia was incorporated.[52] Except during the frenzied years of 1779 and 1784, mechanics had always been lukewarm toward Constitutionalists' efforts to perpetuate test laws which disfranchised former tories or non-jurors, and it is doubtful that they opposed repeal of the laws in 1789.[53] There is evidence that mechanics were wary of the unsuccessful Republican attempts to incorporate the city of Philadelphia in 1783–84, but their doubts were eased by the statute of incorporation proposed in 1789, which established an elected, rather than a self-perpetuating, corporation.[54] Their confidence in the new city government is reflected in their participation in it: in the first election under the new charter, three of the fourteen successful alderman candidates and twelve of the thirty successful common councilman candidates were mechanics.[55]

By 1789, Republican political power was so stable that revision of the state's Constitution of 1776 could be undertaken. The legal amendment procedure, through the Council of Censors, was consciously sidestepped, on the grounds that the whole people had a right to change their government if they saw fit, that conflicts between federal and state constitutions demanded immediate attention, that inherent evils of the government needed repair, and that the Council of Censors was undemocratic.[56] Aware of the sentimental attachment of many Pennsylvanians to the 1776 Constitution, the nationalists put on a magnificently powerful propaganda campaign which suffocated their opponents.[57] The Assembly called a convention in November of 1789 in which Republican strength was so predominant that argumentation was hardly necessary.[58] The instrument which the convention created met most of the Republican requirements: it had a bicameral legislature, a single executive, with a check on the legislature, and a provision for fixing judicial salaries and judicial tenure during good behavior.[59]

Although mechanics had not always befriended the Constitutionalist party in Pennsylvania, there is no evidence that the artisans were ever substantially dissatisfied with the 1776 Constitution which had been the bearing wall of the Constitutionalist party—and an object of Republican criticism—for more than a decade. Yet the manufacturing community voiced no alarm or opposition when Republicans proposed replacing this instrument of government in 1789. The reason is simple: the Republicans did not propose leaving out any of the civil rights and liberties which Pennsylvanians had enjoyed since Independence. In particular, no one proposed undoing universal manhood suffrage, and the right to hold office. The only substantial blow against the democratic radicalism of 1776 was the provision to dispense with the all-powerful unicameral legislature, and from the mechanics' viewpoint this was a worthwhile modification. Too often they had been disappointed by unresponsive legislatures controlled by elements which had no sympathy for their interests.

The new Constitution of Pennsylvania was completed in February of 1790, and was adopted in September of the same year. As in the process of ratification of the United States Constitution, the adoption of the state instrument was without turmoil and struggle, almost without opposition altogether. It was merely the loose end of a revolutionary process which had reached fruition in 1786 and which had been definitively concluded by the ratification of the Constitution of 1787.

ঔঔঔঔঔঔঔঔঔঔঔঔ ঔঔ ঔঔ ঔঔ ঔঔ ঔঔ ঔঔ ঔঔ

Notes to the Chapters

ABBREVIATIONS USED IN THE NOTES

HSP: Historical Society of Pennsylvania
LCP: Library Company of Philadelphia
APS: American Philosophical Society
NYPL: New York Public Library
LC: Library of Congress

I—On the Eve of Revolution

1. Robert Morris to John Hancock, February 4, 1777, Papers of the Continental Congress, No. 137, Appendix, pp. 136–39, Record Group 360, National Archives.

2. Carl and Jessica Bridenbaugh, *Rebels and Gentlemen: Philadelphia in the Age of Franklin* (Philadelphia: Reynel & Hitchcock), 1942, pp. 3–5.

3. For example, "Mercator," *Chronicle,* March 16, 1767; J. P. Brissot de Warville, *New Travels in the United States of America, 1788,* translated by Mara Soceanu Vamos and Durand Echeuerria (Cambridge, Mass.: Harvard University Press, 1964), p. 199; Tench Coxe, *A View of the United States of America* (Philadelphia, 1794; an address originally presented to the Pennsylvania Society for the Encouragement of Manufactures and useful Arts, 1787); "Patrick M'Robert's *Tour through Part of the Northern Provinces of America,*" edited by Carl Bridenbaugh, *Pennsylvania Magazine of History and Biography* 59 (1935):166.

4. Thomas Gage to Lord Shelburne, January 23, 1768, *The Correspondence of General Thomas Gage with the Secretaries of State, 1763–1775,* edited by Clarence Edwin Carter, 2 vols. (New Haven: Yale University Press, 1931, 1933), I, 160–61.

5. Charles M. Andrews, *The Colonial Period of American History,* 4 vols. (New Haven: Yale University Press, 1938), IV, 348–49.

6. Carl Becker, *History of Political Parties in the Province of New York, 1760–1776* (Madison, Wis., 1909), p. 22.

7. Bridenbaugh, *Rebels and Gentlemen,* p. 10.

8. Owen Biddle to David Patterson, August 11, 1771, Owen Biddle Letter Book, 1771, Friends Historical Library, Swarthmore, Pennsylvania.

9. Local furniture-makers enjoyed undisputed control of the Philadelphia market, and the quality of their wares was famous throughout the world by the 1760s, according to Ethel Hall Bjerkoe, *The Cabinetmakers of America* (Garden City, N.J.: Doubleday, 1957), p. 6.

10. Since no census was taken it is difficult to estimate the number of manufacturers in Philadelphia during the Revolution; even the size of the whole population is in dispute; Bridenbaugh, *Cities in Revolt* (New York: Knopf, 1955), p. 216, working from the 1769 and 1774 Tax Lists, estimated it at 40,000, while Sam Bass Warner, *The Private City; Philadelphia in Three Periods of its Growth* (Philadelphia: University of Pennsylvania Press, 1968), pp. 225–26, using both tax records and constables' returns, set the figure at 23,739. Nonetheless, it is clear that mechanics accounted for a very substantial share of the population. A study of the Tax Lists, Bridenbaugh, *Cities in Revolt,* p. 272, showed that of the city's 3,432 listed property owners, 934—about 30 percent—were artisans. An analysis of the callings listed in Francis White, *The Philadelphia Directory* (Philadelphia, 1785), in Charles S. Olton, "Philadelphia Artisans and the American Revolution" (Ph.D. dissertation, University of California at Berkeley, 1968), p. 19, revealed that more than one-third of the household heads listed were mechanics. A Philadelphian alive in 1776 estimated that as much as "one half of the property in the city of Philadelphia [is] owned by men who wear leather aprons," according to the *Evening Post,* March 14, 1776.

II—The Manufacturing Community

1. Quoted in Carl Bridenbaugh, *The Colonial Craftsman* (New York: New York University Press, 1950), p. 156.

2. "A Looker On," *Independent Gazetteer,* January 15, 1785.

3. Charles S. Olton, "Philadelphia's Mechanics in the First Decade of Revolution, 1765–1775," *Journal of American History* 59 (1972):311–14, 325–26.

4. Sam Bass Warner, Jr., *The Private City; Philadelphia in Three Periods of its Growth* (Philadelphia: University of Pennsylvania Press, 1968), pp. 6–7.

5. Richard B. Morris, *Government and Labor in Early America* (New York: Columbia University Press, 1946), p. 49.

6. Quoted in Edward P. Allison and Boies Penrose, *Philadelphia, 1681–1887* (Philadelphia, 1887), p. 20.

7. Ephraim Lipson, *The Economic History of England*, 3 vols. (London: A. & C. Black, Ltd., 1929), I (*The Middle Ages*), 295–96.

8. Thomas Clifford to Lancelot Cowper, December 6, 1768, and Thomas Clifford to John Livingston, June 10, 1769, Thomas Clifford Letter Book, 1767–1773, HSP; John Morgan, *Dissertation on the Reciprocal Advantages of a Perpetual Union between Great-Britain and her American Colonies* (Philadelphia, 1766); [John Baker Holroyd, First Earl of Sheffield], *Observations on the Commerce of the American States* (Philadelphia, 1783); William Smith, D.D., to Dean Tucker, December 18, 1765, William Smith Manuscripts, HSP.

9. John Reynell to Benjamin Lightfoot, April 24, 1770, John Reynell Letter Book, 1770, HSP, reported that Philadelphia bakers usually used "either Negroes or other hands of their own, which they get on low Terms," rather than wage-earners. William Miller and William Coles to William Bradford, March 26, 1781, Bradford Correspondence, HSP, is the record of two journeymen who brought considerable pressure on their employer to pay higher wages. One merchant claimed that only in cabinet-making were the local artisans clearly out of the shadow of the labor shortage. Chaloner and White to Edward Doughty, May 19, 1784, Chaloner and White Letter Book, HSP. The brisk business in the importation of indentured servants in Philadelphia is evidence of the artisans' preference for bound labor. Thomas Gage to Lord Shelburne, January 23, 1768, *The Correspondence of General Thomas Gage with the Secretaries of State, 1763–1775*, edited by Clarence Edwin Carter, 2 vols. (New Haven: Yale University Press, 1931, 1933), I, 161. Employment of wage-earning journeymen became especially slack during the economic recession from 1766 to 1769, according to "A Tradesman," *Chronicle*, December 7, 1767.

10. Jackson T. Main, *The Social Structure of Revolutionary America* (Princeton: Princeton University Press, 1965), pp. 78–81.

11. Victor S. Clark, *History of Manufactures in the United States, 1607–1860* (Washington, D.C., 1916), pp. 22–27. Arthur C. Bining, *British Regulation of the Colonial Iron Industry* (Philadelphia: University of Pennsylvania Press, 1933), p. 158.

12. "Anglus Americanus," *Chronicle*, March 27, 1769.

13. The printing business is one example of such a trade. We have an excellent record of Benjamin Franklin's efforts to find a sponsor in *The Autobiography of Benjamin Franklin*, edited by Lewis Leary (New York: Collier, 1962), pp. 46–48, 66–68. Ward L. Miner, *William Goddard, Newspaperman* (Durham, N.C.: Duke University Press, 1962), pp. 65–66. A few other trades also required extensive capital, but these were the exceptions, not the rule.

14. Clark, *History of Manufactures*, p. 161.

15. Abbot E. Smith, *Colonists in Bondage* (Chapel Hill: University of North Carolina Press, 1947), p. 28.

16. *Mercury and Advertiser,* June 29, 1787.

17. Richard Mason and Parnell Gibbs, Day Book, HSP.

18. Joshua Humphreys to John Dickinson, February 16, 1782, Robert R. Logan Collection, LCP; Remarks on New London, Joshua Humphreys Letter Book, HSP.

19. Newspaper advertisements reveal that partnerships were a common mode of business organization.

20. Minutes of the Friendship Carpenters Company, 1769–1775, APS; The Carpenters Company, Wardens Book, 1769–1781, APS; Minutes of the Tranactions of the Taylors Company of Philadelphia, HSP; and Minutes of the Cordwainers Fire Company, HSP. Some journeymen formed their own organizations. See *Journal,* January 21, 1786, and *Evening Herald,* January 20, 1787. The only organizations which mixed masters and journeymen in their memberships were labor clearing houses. See *Evening Post,* March 16, 1778, *Packet,* May 11, 1784, and "To the Master Taylors," *Evening Herald,* March 29, 1786.

21. For example, a corresponding committee appointed by a mass gathering of artisans in 1774 was composed entirely of master craftsmen. *Gazette,* June 13, 1774. The Patriotic Society, a Revolutionary political organization of mechanics, appears to have restricted its membership to masters. Articles of the Patriotic Society, *Gazette,* August 19, 1772.

22. Francis Hopkinson, *Account of the Grand Federal Procession* (Philadelphia, 1788). Benjamin Rush to Elias Boudinot, July 9, 1788, *Letters of Benjamin Rush,* 2 vols., edited by Lyman H. Butterfield (Princeton: Princeton University Press, 1951), I, 472.

23. Owen Biddle to David Patterson, April 24, 1771, and Owen Biddle to Thomas Wagstaffe, April 24, 1771, Owen Biddle Letter Book, 1771, Friends Historical Library, Swarthmore, Pennsylvania.

24. Warner, *Private City,* pp. 5–7.

25. The statements which follow are based almost entirely on a thorough study of mechanic advertisements in Philadelphia newspapers. Documentation may be found in Charles S. Olton, "Philadelphia Artisans and the American Revolution" (Ph.D. dissertation, University of California at Berkeley, 1968), ch. I.

26. Warner, *Private City,* pp. 17–19.

27. *Ibid.,* pp. 11–14, 17. Joseph Jackson, *Market Street; the Most Historic Highway in America; its Merchants and its Story* (Philadelphia, 1918), chs. I–III. Tax Lists for 1769 and 1774.

28. Raymond B. Clark, "Jonathan Gostelowe (1744–1795), Philadelphia Cabinet Maker" (master's thesis, Winterthur Museum, 1956), p. 113; and Nancy Ann Goyne, "Furniture Craftsmen in Philadelphia, 1760–1780" (master's thesis, Winterthur Museum, 1963), pp. 24–35, 45.

29. Manuscript Declaration of Philadelphia Coopers, 1742, HSP.

30. *Gazette,* March 6, 1766; *Pennsylvania Archives,* 8th Series (Harrisburg, 1935), 6, 5383, 5494, 5539.

31. James H. Hutson, "An Investigation of the Inarticulate: Philadelphia's White Oaks," *William and Mary Quarterly,* 3rd Series, 28 (1971):6–13.

32. *Pennsylvania Archives,* 8th Series, 7, 5833–5834.

33. *Journal,* March 21, 1765.

34. "Navis," *Gazette,* February 16, 1774.

35. The problem came to a head in 1769 because the shoe market was "much overdone"; with sales slow, mechanics were unable to pay high prices for raw materials. Thomas Clifford to Edward and William Gravena, May 23, 1773, Thomas Clifford Letter Book, 1767–1773, HSP. *Pennsylvania Archives,* 8th Series, 7, 6457–58, 6523; 7, 6632.

36. *Pennsylvania Archives,* 8th Series, 7, 6503.

37. "Hint," *Gazette,* July 13, 1769.

38. *Pennsylvania Archives,* 8th Series, 7, 6479, 6503–6504.

39. The petitioners, none of whose names appear in the record, may also have included some artisan tanners (especially in the "Counties adjacent") who depended for their livelihood on leather brokers who brought their goods to market or who supplied them with hides from South Carolina and the hinterland.

40. David MacBride, *An Improved Method of Leather Tanning* (Philadelphia, 1786; originally published in Dublin, 1785).

41. Jonathan Meredith, Shop Book, 1785–1788, and Account of Hides Purchased, 1784–1787, HSP. South Carolina leather could often be imported "on much lower terms than the Tanners sell at," which meant that locally tanned, low-profit leather could be advantageously marketed only in conjunction with a high-profit imported product. Shoemaker and Shurtliff advertisement, *Packet,* June 21, 1783.

42. *Pennsylvania Archives,* 8th Series, 7, 5964.

43. Minutes of the Transactions of the Taylors Company, Article 9, entry for April 7, 1772.

44. Minutes of the Cordwainers Fire Company, entries for March 3, 1760; September 6, 1762; November 9, 1767.

45. There is no evidence to support the claim of Charles H. Lincoln, *The Revolutionary Movement in Pennsylvania* (Philadelphia, 1901), p. 95, that trade guilds were related to attempts by mechanics to expand the franchise.

46. During the years between the founding and dissolution of the Taylors Company, 1771–1776, thirty of the original sixty-eight members resigned. Despite a continual membership drive, the company was able to garner only five new members. Minutes of the Transactions of the Taylors Company, *passim.*

47. *Ibid.,* entries for February 2, 1773; December 6, 1774; June 6, 1775; and October 3, 1775.

48. Minutes of the Cordwainers Fire Company, entry for November 9, 1767.

49. Charles E. Peterson, "American Notes," *Journal of the Society of Architectural Historians* 15 (1956):23–27.

50. For this conclusion I am indebted to Roger W. Moss, Jr., of the Athenaeum of Philadelphia, who has studied in detail the history of the building trades in the eighteenth century.

51. *Articles of the Carpenters Company of Philadelphia, and their Rules for Measuring and Valuing House-Carpenters Work* (Philadelphia, 1786); Articles of Association, 1763, in The Act of Incorporation and By-laws of the Carpenters Company, APS.

52. Minutes of the Friendship Carpenters Company, 1769–1775, APS. The Friendship Company's rules made it possible for its members to under-bid members of the original company.

53. *Ibid.*, entry for July 27, 1775.

54. *Pennsylvania Archives*, 8th Series, 6, 5539.

55. *Ibid.*, 8th Series, 7, 5839; *Gazette*, March 10, 1772; *Pennsylvania Archives*, 8th Series, 7, 5972, 5975, 5986, 6353–54, 6496.

56. Minutes of the Cordwainers Fire Company. Minutes of the Transactions of the Taylors Company.

57. William Cunningham, *The Growth of English Industry and Commerce During the Early Middle Ages* (Cambridge, 1910), pp. 242–43. Lipson, *Economic History of England*, III, 310, 315. *The Cambridge Economic History of Europe*, 6 vols., III (*Economic Organization and Policies in the Middle Ages*), (Cambridge: Cambridge University Press, 1963), 247, 254–55.

58. Warner, *Private City*, p. 8.

III—The Marketplace

1. "A Tradesman," *Chronicle*, October 10, 1768. Anne Bezanson, *Prices and Inflation during the American Revolution: Pennsylvania, 1770–1790* (Philadelphia: University of Pennsylvania Press, 1951), p. 12.

2. Marc Egnal and Joseph A. Ernst, "An Economic Interpretation of the American Revolution," *William and Mary Quarterly*, 3rd Series, 29 (1972): 3, 23, 29.

3. "A Pennsylvania Planter," *Gazette*, August 1, 1771.

4. "A Merchant in Philadelphia" [Charles Thomson] to Benjamin Franklin, June 19, 1765, *Papers of Benjamin Franklin*, ed. Leonard W. Labaree, 14 vols. to date (New Haven: Yale University Press, 1959–1970), XII, 186. Jack M. Sosin, "Imperial Regulation of Colonial Paper Money, 1764–1773," *Pennsylvania Magazine of History and Biography*, 88 (1964):185.

5. "A Tradesman," *Chronicle*, December 7, 1767.

6. Paschall advertisement, *Gazette*, June 14, 1770.

7. The narrative of the conflict is contained in Offley's advertisements, *Journal*, May 8 through July 24, 1766.

8. Thomas Clifford to Samuel Pope, August 1, 1769, Thomas Clifford Letter Book, 1767–73, HSP.

9. Victor S. Clark, *History of Manufactures in the United States, 1607–1860* (Washington, D.C., 1916), p. 151. Jackson T. Main, *The Social Structure of Revolutionary America* (Princeton: Princeton University Press, 1965), p. 83.

10. Harry D. Berg, "The Organization of Business in Colonial Philadelphia," *Pennsylvania History* 10 (1943):157–60. Owen Biddle, Remarks on my accounts, Owen Biddle Letter Book, January, 1780 to July, 1781, Friends Historical Library, Swarthmore, Pennsylvania.

11. "A Mechanic," *Chronicle*, April 16, 1770.

12. *Minutes of the Provincial Council, Pennsylvania Colonial Records* 10, 41. *Gazette*, April 9, 1772. *Pennsylvania Archives*, 8th Series, 8, 6929. Thomas Rodney to Caesar Rodney, September 22, 1772, *Letters to and from Caesar Rodney, 1756–1784*, ed. George Herbert Ryden (Philadelphia: University of Pennsylvania Press, 1933), p. 38.

13. "Philadelphiensis," *Journal*, August 3, 1769.

14. Stiles advertisement, *Gazette* (Supplement), May 4, 1774; Calverley advertisement, *ibid.*, August 28, 1773; Richards advertisement, *ibid.*, December 19, 1771; Shelly advertisement, *ibid.*, August 25, 1768; and Ross advertisement, *Journal*, September 20, 1764.

15. Wood advertisement, *Journal*, October 10, 1771.

16. Fromberger advertisement, *Journal*, September 19, 1771; Cope advertisement, *ibid.*, December 19, 1768; Judah advertisement, *ibid.*, May 8, 1769; and Marie advertisement, *Evening Post*, September 4, 1776.

17. Wood advertisement, *Evening Post*, February 15, 1777.

18. Recently arrived tradesmen, especially those in the clothing trades, frequently advertised that they were "late from London."

19. This was made possible, of course, by the growing practice of employing specialist subcontractors rather than training journeymen.

20. Artisan newspaper advertisements reveal, for example, that some cabinetmakers set up "board yards" behind their shops; some cordwainers tried to beat the raw material problem by curing their own leather; a few brick-layers got control of their raw material source when they began making bricks themselves, and a few stone masons were quarry stone suppliers; several painters, twine-makers, tailors, and hatters also sold both finished wares and their raw materials.

21. Pole advertisement, *Ledger*, January 28, 1775.

22. Wood advertisement, *Journal*, October 10, 1771.

23. Martha Lou Gandy, Joseph Richardson, Quaker Silversmith (master's thesis, Winterthur Museum, 1954), pp. 24–25. Martha G. Fales, *Joseph Richardson & Family: Philadelphia Silversmiths* (Middletown, Conn.: Wesleyan University Press, 1974) was published too late to be consulted for this study.

24. David Hall, *Lately Imported, and to be Sold by David Hall* (Philadelphia, 1765). Thomas and William Bradford, *Imported in the Last Vessels from London* (Philadelphia, 1769). Samuel Coates to Mildred and Roberts, October 27, 1770, Samuel Coates Letter Book, HSP. Thomas Clifford to John Dowele, Clifford Letter Book, 1766–73.

25. Harbeson advertisement, *Journal*, February 22, 1770.

26. Francis White, *The Philadelphia Directory* (Philadelphia, 1785).

27. Flower advertisement, *Gazette*, April 27, 1774.

28. Anthony advertisement, *Journal*, October 4, 1783. Elliott advertisement, *Packet*, March 22, 1773.

29. William Barrell to John Webb, July 21, 1773, Papers of Stephen Collins and Son, XV, LC.

30. Jack Barrell to Jack ———, March 14, 1772, Papers of Stephen Collins, XIII.

31. Wheeler advertisement, *Chronicle*, June 13, 1768. Orr, Dunlope, and Glenholme to Messrs. Greg, Cunningham and Company, November 5, 1768, Orr, Dunlope, and Glenholme Letter Book, HSP. Thomas Frank to Thomas Clifford and Sons, August 3, 1773, Thomas Clifford Correspondence, HSP. Matlack advertisement, *Chronicle*, June 6, 1768.

32. *Chronicle*, August 24, 1774. Ward L. Miner, *William Goddard, Newspaperman* (Durham, N.C.: Duke University Press, 1962), p. 66.

33. Imports and Exports, 1771–1772, to and from the Several Ports in America, Records of the Board of Commissioners for Trade and Plantations (photostat), HSP, lists the principal articles manufactured in Philadelphia and exported by local merchants.

34. John Ramsay, *American Potters and Pottery* (Boston: Houghton Mifflin, 1939), pp. 44–45.

35. *Pennsylvania Archives*, 8th Series, 8, 6616–17. *Journal*, September 27, 1771; January 27 and May 19, 1773; December 7, 1774. *Evening Post*, April 15 and May 20, 1777. *Packet*, March 22 and August 30, 1773; February 27, 1775.

36. Egnal and Ernst, "Economic Interpretation," *William and Mary Quarterly*, 3rd Series, 29 (1972):29.

37. "Colonus," *Chronicle*, March 13, 1769; "Anglus Americanus," *ibid.*, March 27, 1769.

38. Wistar advertisement, *Gazette*, September 26, 1765.

39. Jackson advertisement, *ibid.*, October 16, 1766.

40. [John Dickinson], *The Late Regulations Respecting the British Colonies* (Philadelphia, 1765).

41. Thomas Wharton to Benjamin Franklin, April 27, 1765, *Papers of Benjamin Franklin*, ed. Labaree, XII, 113.

42. Non-Importation Resolutions, December 25, 1765, Collectanea of Jonah

Thompson, VII, 158, HSP. The only foreign goods exempted from the restriction were dye stuffs and "Utensils necessary for carrying on Manufactures."

43. William Smith, D.D., to Dean Tucker, December 18, 1765, William Smith Manuscripts, HSP.

44. Egnal and Ernst, "Economic Interpretation," *William and Mary Quarterly*, 3rd Series, 29 (1972):3, 32.

45. Rutherford advertisement, *Journal*, June 20, 1765.

46. Mause advertisement, *Gazette*, May 1, 1766.

47. *Gazette*, May 22 and July 9, 1766. Thomas Wharton to Benjamin Franklin, May 22, 1766, *Papers of Benjamin Franklin*, ed. Labaree, XIII, 282.

48. "Oeconomicus," *Chronicle*, January 4, 1769.

49. Mason advertisement, *ibid.*, December 11, 1768.

50. Mason advertisement, *ibid.*, November 6, 1769.

51. *Minutes of the Common Council of the City of Philadelphia, 1704–1776* (Philadelphia, 1847), pp. 745, 754.

52. Kennedy advertisement, *Chronicle*, December 5, 1768.

53. Barge, Morgan, White, and Reno advertisement, *Chronicle*, July 24, 1769.

54. Evans advertisement, *Gazette*, October 18, 1770.

55. *From the Merchants and Traders of Philadelphia . . . to the Merchants and Manufacturers of Great Britain* [broadside edition of the 1768 non-importation agreement], (Philadelphia, 1770). *The Following Address Was Read at a Meeting of the Merchants, at the Lodge in Philadelphia, on Monday, the 25th of April, 1768* (Philadelphia, 1768).

56. *To the Tradesmen, Farmers, and Other Inhabitants of the City and County of Philadelphia* (Philadelphia, September 24, 1770).

57. They were not, however, altogether successful. Alexander MacKraby to Sir Philip Francis, January 1, 1770, "Philadelphia Society before the Revolution," *Pennsylvania Magazine of History and Biography* 11 (1887):492.

58. "Colonus," *Journal*, January 12, 1769.

59. Samuel Coates to William Logan, September 26, 1770, Samuel Coates Letter Book, HSP. Henry Drinker to Philip Laurens, August 3, 1773, Henry Drinker Letter Book, 1772–86, HSP.

60. The gross sales of the manufactory during a one-year period at the height of the business were £955 12s 1d. Miers Fisher Ledger, HSP.

61. *Journal*, March 12, 1767.

62. *Gazette*, March 8 and November 8, 1770; November 14, 1771. *Pennsylvania Archives*, 8th Series, 8, 6684–86. The undertaking lost money and never attained the success Franklin and other promoters had hoped for.

63. *Gazette*, March 23, 1773.

64. *A Number of the Inhabitants of this City* . . . (Philadelphia, 1765). *Gazette*, January 9, 1766. Thomas Wharton to Benjamin Franklin, April 26, 1766, *Papers of Benjamin Franklin*, ed. Labaree, XIII, 252. On the eve of Independence, another linen manufactory was attempted, in which mechanics played a major role. *Ledger*, March 11, March 18, and March 29, 1775.

65. "A Hint to the Public," *Chronicle*, February 25, 1771. "An Hibernian," *ibid.*, March 4, 1771. "Jason," *ibid.*, March 11, 1771. "An Hibernian," *ibid.*, March 17, November 11, and November 25, 1771.

66. Charles Thomson, "General Maxims of Trade," Charles Thomson Memorandum Book, 1754–74, Letters of Charles Thomson, HSP.

67. Thomas Clifford to Lancelot Cowper, June 21, 1769, Thomas Clifford Letter Book, 1767–73, HSP. John Dickinson, *Letters from a Farmer in Pennsylvania to the Inhabitants of the British Colonies* (New York, 1768), Letter II, made note of Pennsylvanians' manufacturing activity, but criticized them for not making a sufficient commitment to it.

68. Benjamin Rush to ————, January 26, 1769, dated from London, *Letters of Benjamin Rush*, ed. Lyman H. Butterfield, 2 vols. (Princeton, 1951), I, 74–75.

69. The merchants who had adopted favorable attitudes toward manufacturing in this crisis period sustained their interests, which eventually culminated in the formation of the "United Company of Philadelphia for Promoting American Manufactures and useful Arts," in 1775. *Gazette* (Supplement), February 22, 1775.

70. "A Citizen," *Journal*, October 11, 1770.

71. *Chronicle*, November 22, 1771.

72. See, for example, Wood advertisement, *Gazette* (Supplement), January 23, 1772, and the introductory statement in *Mercury*, April 7, 1775.

IV—The Emergence of the Mechanics in Politics, 1765–70

1. Charles H. Lincoln, *The Revolutionary Movement in Pennsylvania* (Philadelphia, 1901), pp. 78, 86.

2. Charles S. Olton, "Philadelphia's Mechanics in the First Decade of Revolution, 1765–1775," *Journal of American History* 59 (1972):311–14.

3. Mount Regale Fishing Company Papers, HSP. Register of the Jockey Club, HSP. *Chronicle*, May 10, 1773. One mechanic, William Pollard, a carpenter, belonged to the Jockey Club.

4. See, for example, Ledger Belonging to the Delaware Fire Company [Ledger of the King George the Third Fire Company], HSP: Minute Book of the Delaware Fire Company, HSP; Minutes of the Union Fire Company, Commencing the 7th Day of December, 1736, 2 vols., I, LCP; and Ledger of the Hibernia Fire Company, HSP.

5. The only notable exception was the Society of the Friendly Sons of St.

Patrick, whose members were, for the most part, men of wealth and social distinction who were of Irish descent.

6. *The Constitution and Rules of the St. Andrews Society in Philadelphia* (Philadelphia, 1769). *An Historical Catalogue of the St. Andrews Society of Philadelphia, 1749–1781* (Philadelphia, 1882), pp. 53–93. Society of the Sons of St. George, Minutes, HSP.

7. The Society of the Sons of St. George, Minutes.

8. Carl and Jessica Bridenbaugh, *Rebels and Gentlemen; Philadelphia in the Age of Franklin* (Philadelphia: Reynal & Hitchcock, 1942), pp. 336–38.

9. E. V. Lamberton, "Colonial Libraries of Pennsylvania," *Pennsylvania Magazine of History and Biography* 42 (1918):204–206.

10. David Hawke, *In the Midst of a Revolution* (Philadelphia: University of Pennsylvania Press, 1961), p. 44.

11. James H. Hutson, *Pennsylvania Politics, 1746–1776; the Movement for Royal Government and its Consequences* (Princeton: Princeton University Press, 1972), p. 181.

12. *Pennsylvania Archives* (Harrisburg, 1935), 8th Series, 7, 5964, 5972, 5975, 5986. Two subsequent bills failed for the same reason; *ibid.*, 7, 6353–54, 6496.

13. Richard Peters to Jasper Yates, November 26, 1765, Yates Correspondence, HSP. William S. Hanna, *Benjamin Franklin and Pennsylvania Politics* (Stanford: Stanford University Press, 1964), pp. 169–70. Hutson, *Pennsylvania Politics,* pp. 210–11.

14. Hanna, *Benjamin Franklin and Pennsylvania Politics,* p. 52.

15. Hutson, *Pennsylvania Politics,* pp. 73–83, 172.

16. Olton, "Philadelphia's Mechanics in the First Decade of Revolution," *Journal of American History* 59 (1972):311–12. Hutson, *Pennsylvania Politics,* pp. 73–83, 172.

17. Hutson, *Pennsylvania Politics,* pp. 192–94, 198–99.

18. Benjamin H. Newcomb, "Effects of the Stamp Act on Colonial Pennsylvania Politics," *William and Mary Quarterly,* 3rd Series, 23 (1966):261–64. Letters of John Hughes and Joseph Galloway to Benjamin Franklin, *Papers of Benjamin Franklin,* ed. Leonard Labaree, 14 vols., to date (New Haven: Yale University Press, 1959–1972), XII, 266, 373–74; XIII, 285.

19. Quoted in Francis Von A. Cabeen, "The Society of the Sons of St. Tammany of Philadelphia," *Pennsylvania Magazine of History and Biography* 25 (1901):439.

20. James H. Hutson, "An Investigation of the Inarticulate: Philadelphia's White Oaks," *William and Mary Quarterly,* 3rd Series, 28 (1971):7–9.

21. Joseph Galloway to William Franklin, November 14, 1765, *Papers of Benjamin Franklin,* ed. Labaree, XII, 373. Samuel Wharton to Benjamin Franklin, October 13, 1765, *ibid.,* XII, 316.

22. Benjamin Rush to Ebenezer Hazard, November 8, 1765, *Letters of*

Benjamin Rush, 2 vols., ed. Lyman H. Butterfield (Princeton: Princeton University Press, 1951), I, 18.

23. *Chronicle,* September 30, 1771.

24. Charles Thomson to Messrs. Welsh, Wilkinson & Co., November 7, 1765, *Collections of the New-York Historical Society* 11 (1878):5.

25. Non-Importation Resolutions, December 25, 1765, Collectanea of Jonah Thompson, VII, 158, HSP. At least 34 of the 236 who signed the document were mechanics.

26. Carl L. Becker, *The History of Political Parties in the Province of New York, 1760–1776* (Madison, Wis., 1909), p. 22. The same thesis was posited eight years before Becker's famous formulation by Lincoln, *Revolutionary Movement,* p. 78.

27. David L. Jacobson, *John Dickinson and the Revolution in Pennsylvania, 1764–1776* (Berkeley and Los Angeles: University of California Press, 1965), pp. 59–60. The Assembly did not respond to the Massachusetts Circular Letter. *Pennsylvania Archives,* 8th Series, 7, 6181–82, 6188.

28. *Minutes of the Common Council of the City of Philadelphia, 1704–1776* (Philadelphia, 1847), pp. 725–26 (entry for December 22, 1767). The Common Council, unlike the Assembly, had the courtesy to reply to Massachusetts.

29. Hutson, *Pennsylvania Politics,* pp. 210, 211.

30. *Ibid.,* pp. 214, 220.

31. John J. Zimmerman, "Charles Thomson, 'The Sam Adams of Philadelphia,'" *Mississippi Valley Historical Review* 45 (1958):472–73.

32. "Talionis," *Chronicle,* August 6, 1771. Henry Drinker to Abel James, April 29, 1770, "The Effects of the 'Non-Importation Agreement' in Philadelphia, 1769–1770," *Pennsylvania Magazine of History and Biography* 14 (1890):42.

33. *Ibid.*

34. "A Tradesman," *Chronicle,* October 10, 1768.

35. Thomas Gage to Lord Barrington, May 13, 1768, *The Correspondence of General Thomas Gage, with the Secretaries of State, 1763–1775,* 2 vols., ed. Clarence E. Carter (New Haven: Yale University Press, 1931–33), II, 468.

36. John Reynell to Mildred & Roberts, May 17, 1769, Reynell Letter Book, May, 1769 to November, 1770, HSP. Reynell reiterated this opinion throughout 1769 to other correspondents.

37. Robert L. Brunhouse, "The Effect of the Townshend Acts in Pennsylvania," *Pennsylvania Magazine of History and Biography* 54 (1930):360. *Gazette,* May 7, 1770. Thomas Fisher to the Committee of Merchants, July 7, 1769, and "Non-Importation, 1770," Joshua and Thomas Fisher Papers, HSP. Henry Drinker to Abel James, April 29, 1770, "Effects of the 'Non-Importation Agreement,'" *Pennsylvania Magazine of History and Biography* 14 (1890):42.

38. "A. B.," *Chronicle,* January 29, 1770.

39. *Chronicle,* July 24, 1769. *Gazette,* July 20, 1769.

40. *Gazette,* January 25, 1770. Henry Drinker to Abel James, December 9, 1769, "The Effects of the 'Non-Importation Agreement,'" *Pennsylvania Magazine of History and Biography* 14 (1890):41.

41. *Chronicle,* May 7, 1770.

42. *Ibid.,* May 28, 1770.

43. "Tradesman," *Chronicle,* May 21, 1770. "Queries Read at Davenport's Tavern, 1770," Joshua and Thomas Fisher Papers, HSP.

44. *To the Free and Patriotic Inhabitants of the City of Philad. and Province of Pennsylvania* (Philadelphia, May 31, 1770).

45. "Tradesman," *Chronicle,* May 21, 1770.

46. *Ibid.*

47. "Libertas et Natale Solum," *Chronicle,* June 4, 1770. *To the Free and Patriotic Inhabitants of the City of Philad. and Province of Pennsylvania* (Philadelphia, May 31, 1770).

48. Samuel Coates to William Logan, September 26, 1770, Samuel Coates Letter Book, HSP. "Read at the Coffee House in the Summer, 1770," Fisher Papers, HSP. This was a standard merchant view.

49. "A Spectator," *Gazette,* June 14, 1770.

50. "A House Carpenter," *Chronicle,* June 18, 1770.

51. *Journal,* June 7, 1770.

52. Samuel Coates to William Logan, September 26, 1770, Samuel Coates Letter Book, HSP. John Adams, *Diary, The Adams Papers,* 1st Series, 4 vols., ed. Lyman H. Butterfield (Cambridge, Mass.: Harvard University Press, 1961), II, 115. Franklin's letter was published in *Journal,* May 10, 1770.

53. *Journal,* July 5, 1770.

54. "Publicola," *Chronicle,* January 26, 1767. "Q.Z.," and "A.B.," and "Mercator," *Chronicle,* March 16, 1767. "Wrote in 1770," Fisher Papers, HSP. Ralph D. Gray, "Philadelphia and the Chesapeake and Delaware Canal, 1769–1823," *Pennsylvania Magazine of History and Biography* 84 (1960):401–23.

55. *To the Public* (Philadelphia, October 3, 1770). *To the Freeholders, Merchants, Tradesmen and Farmers of the City and County of Philad.* (Philadelphia, September 26, 1770). Samuel Coates to William Logan, September 26, 1770, Samuel Coates Letter Book, HSP.

56. *Chronicle,* September 24 and October 1, 1770.

57. *To the Public* (Philadelphia, October 3, 1770).

58. *Chronicle,* September 24, 1770.

59. *To the Tradesmen, Farmers, and other Inhabitants of the City and County of Philadelphia* (Philadelphia, September 24, 1770).

60. "A Citizen," *Chronicle,* October 11, 1770.

61. *Gazette,* October 4, 1770. *Philadelphia, Thursday, September 27, 1770. Many Respectable Freeholders* . . . (Philadelphia, September 27, 1770).

62. Alexander Graydon, *Memoirs of His Own Times with Reminiscences of the Men and Events*, ed. John S. Littell (Philadelphia, 1846), p. 122. Graydon used the term in 1774.

V—Mechanics in the Ascendency, 1770–74

1. Judith M. Diamondstone, "Philadelphia's Municipal Corporation, 1701–1776," *Pennsylvania Magazine of History and Biography* 90 (1966):183, 193, 201.

2. *Chronicle*, May 15, 1769. "Tom Trudge," *ibid.*, March 27, 1769. "A Citizen," *ibid.*, September 18, 1769. "Uptown," *ibid.*, October 2, 1769.

3. Charles S. Olton, "Philadelphia's First Environmental Crisis," *Pennsylvania Magazine of History and Biography* 98 (1974):97–98.

4. *To the Worthy Tradesmen, Artificers, Mechanics &c. Electors for the City and County of Philadelphia* (Philadelphia, October 1, 1770).

5. James Claypoole advertisement, Benjamin Armitage advertisement, and Benjamin Humphreys advertisement, *Gazette* (Supplement), September 22, 1773. It was customary to advertise one's candidacy for the office of sheriff and coroner, but not for the other provincial or municipal offices.

6. Enoch Story advertisement, *ibid.*

7. Election results were published in all Philadelphia newspapers during the first week of October each year.

8. For the traditional view, see Charles H. Lincoln, *The Revolutionary Movement in Pennsylvania* (Philadelphia, 1901), p. 78; and J. Paul Selsam, *The Pennsylvania Constitution of 1776: A Study in Revolutionry Democracy* (Philadelphia: University of Pennsylvania Press, 1936), p. 33.

9. Thomas Paine, "A Serious Address to the People of Pennsylvania on the Present Situation of their Affairs," *The Complete Writings of Thomas Paine*, ed. Philip S. Foner, 2 vols. (New York: Citadel Press, 1945), II, 287–288.

10. Thomas Wharton to Benjamin Franklin, ———, 1965, *The Papers of Benjamin Franklin*, 14 vols., to date, ed. Leonard W. Labaree (New Haven: Yale University Press, 1959–72), XII, 356–57. "The Plan &c.," *Gazette*, November 9, 1774.

11. "A Brother Chip," *Gazette*, September 27, 1770.

12. *Ibid.*

13. "A Brother to the Bretheren of the Chip," *Chronicle*, October 1, 1770.

14. Joseph Galloway to Benjamin Franklin, September 27, 1770, quoted by Hutson, "An Investigation of the Inarticulate: Philadelphia's White Oaks," *William and Mary Quarterly*, 3rd Series, 28 (1971):22.

15. James H. Hutson, *Pennsylvania Politics, 1746–1776; the Movement for*

Royal Government and Its Consequences (Princeton: Princeton University Press, 1972), p. 230.

16. *Fellow Citizens and Countrymen* (Philadelphia, October 1, 1770). Parker was re-elected in 1771 and 1772.

17. *Gazette*, May 21, 1770.

18. "A Citizen of Philadelphia," *ibid.*, September 22, 1773. Samuel Coates to William Logan, December 10, 1770, Samuel Coates Letter Book, HSP.

19. Ward L. Miner, *William Goddard, Newspaperman* (Durham, N.C.: Duke University Press, 1962), ch. V.

20. John J. Zimmerman, "Benjamin Franklin and the Pennsylvania *Chronicle*," *Pennsylvania Magazine of History and Biography* 81 (1957):353.

21. *The Partnership: or the History of the Rise and Progress of the Pennsylvania Chronicle* (Philadelphia, 1770).

22. Miner, *William Goddard*, pp. 108–109.

23. See, for example, *Journal*, July 28, August 4 and 11, 1768.

24. "A Country Farmer," *Chronicle*, August 22, 1768.

25. *Ibid.*, March 30, 1772. "The Address of a Number of Freemen . . . ," *ibid.*, October 24, 1772.

26. *Ibid.*

27. *Ibid.*

28. Articles of the Patriotic Society, *Gazette*, August 19, 1772.

29. "Publius," *Chronicle*, September 5, 1772.

30. *Ibid.*

31. *Ibid.*

32. *A Tradesman's Address to his Countrymen* (Philadelphia, March 2, 1772). "The Address of a Number of Freemen . . . ," *Chronicle*, October 24, 1772.

33. "A Citizen of Philadelphia," *Gazette*, September 22, 1773.

34. Articles of the Patriotic Society, *ibid.*, August 19, 1772.

35. "A Citizen of Philadelphia," *ibid.*, September 22, 1773.

36. "A Mechanic," *Chronicle*, September 27, 1773.

37. "Pacificus," *ibid.*, September 20, 1773. "A Mechanic," *ibid.*, September 27, 1773.

38. "A Mechanic," *ibid.*, September 27, 1773.

39. "A Mechanic," *ibid.*, December 3, 1773.

40. *Ibid.*, January 3, 1774.

41. Thomas Wharton to Samuel Wharton, November 24, 1773, and Thomas Wharton to Thomas Walpole, December 21, 1773, Thomas Wharton Letter Book, 1773–84, HSP.

42. *A Card* (Philadelphia, December 2, 1773).

43. *Gazette,* December 29, 1773. Thomas Wharton to Thomas Walpole, December 27, 1773, Wharton Letter Book, 1773–84.

44. *Gazette,* August 17, 1774.

45. Charles Thomson to David Ramsay, November 4, 1786, "The Thomson Papers," *Collections of the New York Historical Society* 11 (1878):219.

46. Thomas Mifflin to Samuel Adams, May 21, 1774, Samuel Adams Papers, NYPL.

47. Charles Thomson to William Henry Drayton, no date, "Thomson Papers," *Collections of New York Historical Society* 11 (1878):280–81.

48. "Joseph Reed's Narrative," *Collections of the New York Historical Society* 11 (1878):269–71.

49. Thomas Wharton to ———, May 31, 1774, Wharton Letter Book, 1773–84, HSP.

50. *Ibid.*

51. Charles Thomson to David Ramsay, November 4, 1786, "Thomson Papers," *Collections of the New York Historical Society* 11 (1878):220.

52. William Smith, Notes and Papers on the Commencement of the American Revolution, William Smith Manuscripts, 1765–74, HSP.

53. *Gazette,* June 15, 1774. Thomson to Ramsay, November 4, 1786, "Thomson Papers," *Collections of the New York Historical Society* 11 (1878):222. *To the Manufacturers and Mechanics of Philadelphia, the Northern Liberties, and District of Southwark* (Philadelphia, June 8, 1774).

54. *Extracts of the Diary of Christopher Marshall kept at Philadelphia and Lancaster during the American Revolution, 1774–1781,* ed. William Duane (Albany, N.Y., 1877), p. 7 (entry for June 10, 1774).

55. *Gazette,* June 15, 1774.

56. The Mechanics to John Dickinson, June 27, 1774, Robert R. Logan Collection, LCP. The names of the tradesmen who wrote this exceptionally important and long overlooked document are unknown. See also, Minutes of the Committee, Du Simitière Papers, HSP (entry for July 8).

57. The Mechanics to John Dickinson, June 27, 1774, Logan Collection, LCP. *Gazette,* June 15, 1774.

58. *At a Meeting at the Philosophical Society's Hall* (Philadelphia, June 10, 1774). Charles Thomson, Notes on a Meeting of a Number of Gentlemen, Convened on the 10 June, 1774, Charles Thomson Memorandum Book, 1754–74, HSP.

59. Thomson to Drayton, "Thomson Papers," *Collections of New York Historical Society* 11 (1878):287.

60. Charles Thomson, Notes on a Meeting of a Number of Gentlemen, Thomson Memorandum Book, 1754–74, HSP.

61. The Mechanics to John Dickinson, June 27, 1774, Logan Collection, LCP.

62. *At a Meeting at the Philosophical Society's Hall* (Philadelphia, June 10, 1774). The Mechanics to John Dickinson, June 27, 1774, Logan Collection, LCP.

63. "Wrote in 1774," Joshua and Thomas Fisher Papers, HSP.

64. The Mechanics to John Dickinson, June 27, 1774, Logan Collection, LCP.

65. Thomson to Drayton, "Thomson Papers," *Collections of New York Historical Society* 11 (1878):279.

66. Minutes of a Meeting, 1774, Dickinson Papers, HSP. The Mechanics to John Dickinson, June 27, 1774, Logan Collection, LCP.

67. Thomson to Ramsay, November 4, 1786, "Thomson Papers," *Collections of New York Historical Society* 11 (1878):223.

68. The Mechanics to John Dickinson, June 27, 1774, Logan Collection, LCP.

69. Henry Drinker to B. Booth, June 21, 1774, Henry Drinker Letter Book, 1772–86, HSP.

70. The Mechanics to John Dickinson, June 27, 1774, Logan Collection, LCP. William Smith, Notes and Papers on the Commencement of the American Revolution, William Smith Manuscripts, 1765–74, HSP.

VI—Independence and Radical Politics, 1774–76

1. Gunning Bedford, Francis Wade, Jacob Rush, Thomas Affleck, Joseph Wetherill, Jacob Morgan, and Plunket Fleeson to the Committee at Philadelphia, July 8, 1774, Minutes of the Committee, Du Simitière Papers, HSP.

2. The Mechanics to John Dickinson, June 27, 1774, Robert R. Logan Collection, LCP.

3. Charles Thomson to William Henry Drayton, no date, *Collections of the New York Historical Society* 11 (1878):279.

4. The Mechanics to John Dickinson, June 27, 1774, Logan Collection, LCP.

5. Charles Thomson to William Henry Drayton, no date, *Collections of New York Historical Society* 11 (1878):279. *Pennsylvania Archives*, 8th Series (Harrisburg, 1935), 8, 7085–92, 7097–101. There were no Indian disturbances at the time.

6. Minutes of the Committee (entry for July 8, 1774), Du Simitière Papers, HSP.

7. Bedford, *et al.*, to the Committee at Philadelphia, July 8, 1774, Minutes of the Committee, Du Simitière Papers, HSP.

8. Thomas Willing, Chairman, on behalf of the Committee, to the Mechanics, July 11, 1774, Minutes of the Committee, Du Simitière Papers, HSP.

9. "Russel," *Gazette*, July 20, 1774. Italics in original.

10. "An Artisan," *ibid.*, August 31, 1774. See also, "A Mechanic," *Packet,* September 5, 1774.

11. Post Script, The Mechanics to John Dickinson, June 27, 1774, Logan Collection, LCP [apparently added July 4, 1774].

12. *Pennsylvania Archives,* 8th Series, 7, 7100.

13. "A Card," *Gazette,* September 7, 1774.

14. Silas Deane to Mrs. Deane, September 5–6, 1774, *Letters of Members of the Continental Congress,* ed. Edmund C. Burnett, 8 vols. (Washington, D.C.: The Carnegie Institution, 1921–36), I, 11.

15. Thomas Willing, Chairman, on behalf of the Committee, to the Mechanics, July 11, 1774, Minutes of the Committee, Du Simitière Papers.

16. The Mechanics to John Dickinson, June 27, 1774, Logan Collection.

17. The Pennsylvania Assembly recognized the edict of Congress, and although it recommended "a strict attention to, and inviolable Observation of" the non-intercourse policy it had so warmly opposed, nevertheless, as the legal government of the colony, it could not enforce this extra-legal regulation. For this reason, committee-government continued to thrive. *Pennsylvania Archives,* 8th Series, 8, 7162.

18. "To the Public," *Gazette,* November 2, 1774.

19. *Ibid.,* November 9, 1774.

20. *Ibid.*

21. "The Plan, &c,," *Gazette,* November 9, 1774.

22. *Packet,* November 14, 1774.

23. Richard A. Ryerson, "Leadership in Crisis; Radical Committees of Philadelphia and the Coming of the Revolution in Pennsylvania, 1765–1776: A Study in the Revolutionary Process, (Ph.D. thesis, Johns Hopkins University, 1972), p. 258.

24. *Gazette,* November 16, 1774. Ryerson, "Leadership in Crisis," p. 469 [Table XXXI].

25. *Gazette,* November 16, 1774.

26. Ryerson, "Leadership in Crisis," p. 342.

27. Henry Drinker to Captain John Harper, July 18, 1775, Henry Drinker Letter Book, 1772–86, HSP.

28. *Gazette,* August 23, 1775. Charles Thomson to William Henry Drayton, no date, *Collections of New York Historical Society* 11 (1878):283.

29. George Cuthbert to Lieutenant-General John Dalling, April, 1775, *Pennsylvania Magazine of History and Biography* 66 (1942):206.

30. *Committee for the City of Phildelphia, to be and Continue until the 16th day of February A.D. 1776* . . . (Philadelphia, 1775) [Ms. note on the original copy, LCP].

31. Ryerson, "Leadership in Crisis," p. 386 (Table XXVIII).

32. *Extracts from the Diary of Christopher Marshall, kept in Philadelphia and Lancaster during the American Revolution,* ed. William Duane (Albany, N.Y., 1877), 14 (entry for February 17, 1775).

33. *Evening Post,* September 14, and 19, 1775.

34. *Ibid.,* February 1, 1776.

35. "Extracts from the Diary of Dr. James Clitherall, 1776," *Pennsylvania Magazine of History and Biography* 22 (1898):471.

36. The other two, James Cannon, a university professor, and Dr. Thomas Young, a physician, had no apparent ties with the artisans. John Adams, *Diary, The Adams Papers,* ed. Lyman H. Butterfield (Cambridge, Mass.: Harvard University Press, 1961), 1st Series, III, 331, 222.

37. *Gazette,* February 21, 1776.

38. Ryerson, "Leadership in Crisis," pp. 441–42.

39. Of the four radical candidates in the May Assembly election, none was a mechanic and only one was elected, a poor showing for both mechanics and extreme radicals generally, in light of their success in capturing the Philadelphia Committee in February. *Gazette,* May 1, 1776. David Hawke, *In the Midst of a Revolution* (Philadelphia: University of Pennsylvania Press, 1961), p. 19.

40. "An Elector," *Packet,* April 29, 1776.

41. "An Elector," *Gazette,* May 1, 1776.

42. "An Elector," *ibid.,* May 15, 1776.

43. Thomas Paine, "A Serious Address to the People of Pennsylvania on the Present Situation of their Affairs," *The Complete Writings of Thomas Paine,* ed. Philip S. Foner, 2 vols. (New York: Citadel Press, 1945), II, 287–88.

44. *Gazette,* May 15, 1776.

45. *Ibid.,* June 26, 1776. *To the People* (Philadelphia, 1776). *Philadelphia, May 20* (Philadelphia, May 20, 1776).

46. "Extracts from the Diary of Dr. James Clitherall, 1776," *Pennsylvania Magazine of History and Biography* 22 (1898):470. *Proceedings of the Provincial Conference of Committees of the Province of Pennsylvania* (Philadelphia, 1776).

47. *Extracts from the Diary of Christopher Marshall,* ed. Duane, 81 (entry for July 3, 1776).

48. Hawke, *In the Midst of a Revolution,* p. 174. *Proceedings of the Provincial Conference of Committees* (Philadelphia, 1776).

49. *Packet,* November 26, 1776.

50. "A Dialogue," *Ledger,* October 12, and 26, 1776. Sarah Yates to Jasper Yates, September 14, 1776, Yates Papers, HSP. Except for David Rittenhouse, no Philadelphia mechanic was elected.

51. *The Constitution of the Commonwealth of Pennsylvania* (Philadelphia, 1776).

52. "An Associator," *Evening Post,* October 28, 1778.

53. *Ibid.,* October 22, 1776. *At a Meeting Held at the Philosophical Society Hall* . . . (Philadelphia, October 17, 1776). *Extracts from the Diary of Christopher Marshall,* ed. Duane, p. 103 [entry for November 8, 1776].

54. Silas Deane to Simeon Deane, 1779, *Pennsylvania Magazine of History and Biography* 17 (1893):348.

55. Alexander Graydon, *Memoirs of His Own Times with Reminiscences of the Men and Events,* ed. John S. Littell (Philadelphia, 1846), p. 285.

56. *Extracts from the Diary of Christopher Marshall,* ed. Duane, 102 (entry for November 5, 1776).

57. Thomas Paine to Henry Laurens, January 14, 1779, *The Complete Writings of Thomas Paine,* ed. Foner, II, 1164.

58. Paul Selsam, *The Pennsylvania Constitution of 1776; A Study in Revolutionary Democracy* (Philadelphia: University of Pennsylvania Press, 1936), pp. 235–36, 241. In a special election during February of 1777, the friends of the government won all the city's Assembly seats.

59. *Gazette,* June 18, 1777.

60. *Ibid.,* March 26 and April 9, 1777. *To the Freeholders and Independent Electors of Philadelphia* (Philadelphia, November 5, 1776).

61. *Ledger,* September 7, 1776.

VII—The Fortunes of War, 1776–83

1. J. Paul Selsam, *The Pennsylvania Constitution of 1776; a Study in Revolutionary Democracy* (Philadelphia: University of Pennsylvania Press, 1936), Ch. V.

2. Anne Bezanson, *Prices and Inflation during the American Revolution: Philadelphia, 1770–1790* (Philadelphia: University of Pennsylvania Press, 1951), pp. 11, 17.

3. Richard Humphreys advertisement, *Evening Post,* February 27, 1779. Jacob Hiltzheimer, *Extracts from the Diary of Jacob Hiltzheimer,* ed. Jacob Cox Parsons (Philadelphia 1893), 41 (entry for October 5, 1779). Lock factory advertisement, *Ledger,* April 13, 1776.

4. E. James Ferguson, *The Power of the Purse: A History of American Public Finance, 1776–1790* (Chapel Hill: University of North Carolina Press, 1961), ch. I.

5. "A Citizen of Philadelphia," *Gazette,* January 10, 1781.

6. Ferguson, *Power of the Purse,* pp. 13, 16, 19.

7. Stephen Paschall, Ledger C, 1758–89, HSP. Bezanson, *Prices and Inflation,* pp. 12–13.

8. *Extracts from the Diary of Christopher Marshall kept at Philadelphia and Lancaster during the American Revolution,* ed. William Duane (Albany, New York, 1898), p. 210 (entry for January 10, 1779).

9. Richard B. Morris, *Government and Labor in Early America* (New York: Columbia University Press, 1946), pp. 92–110.

10. *Gazette,* April 7, 1779.

11. "An Address of the Committee of the City and Liberties of Philadelphia . . . ," *Evening Post,* June 29, 1779.

12. *Evening Post,* May 29, 1779.

13. "An Address to the Committee of the City and Liberties of Philadelphia . . . ," *Evening Post,* June 29, 1779.

14. *At a General Meeting of the Citizens of Philadelphia and Parts Adjacent . . .* (Philadelphia, May 25, 1779). *Packet,* May 27 and July 3, 1779. "An Address of the Committee . . . , *Evening Post,* June 6, 1779.

15. *The Independent and Constitutional Ticket . . .* (Philadelphia, [1779]).

16. *To the Inhabitants of Pennsylvania* (Philadelphia, July 11, 1779). Tanners, curriers, shoemakers, and cordwainers were included in the group.

17. "A Whig Shoemaker," *Packet,* July 15, 1779.

18. *Evening Post,* August 5, 1779. The radical committee polled 2115 votes, while the "contrary Ticket" received a mere 281.

19. *Packet,* July 29, and July 31, 1779.

20. *Extracts from the Journal of Elizabeth Drinker,* ed., Henry D. Biddle (Philadelphia, 1889), p. 116 (entries for May 22 and May 24, 1779).

21. *Ibid.,* pp. 116–18 [entries for May 22 through June 26, *passim.*]. *Extracts from the Diary of Christopher Marshall,* ed. Duane, 218 (entry for May 28, 1779).

22. *Pennsylvania Archives,* 1st Series, 12 volumes (Harrisburg, 1852–56), 7, 392.

23. "A Citizen of Philadelphia," *Packet,* September 30, 1779.

24. *Pennsylvania Archives,* 1st Series, 7, 394.

25. Benjamin Rush to Charles Lee, October 24, 1779, *Letters of Benjamin Rush,* 2 vols., ed. Lyman H. Butterfield (Princeton: Princeton University Press, 1951), I, 240, 244.

26. Frederick O. Stone, "Philadelphia Society One Hundred Years Ago, or the Reign of Continental Money," *Pennsylvania Magazine of History and Biography* 3 (1879):383–84.

27. Sam Bass Warner, *The Private City; Philadelphia in Three Periods of its Growth* (Philadelphia: University of Pennsylvania Press, 1968), pp. 42–43.

28. *Packet,* September 25, 1779.

29. *Ibid.,* July 1, 1779. "Journal of Samuel Rowland Fisher, of Philadelphia, 1779–1781, ed., Anna Wharton Morris, *Pennsylvania Magazine of History and Biography* 41 (1917):168–69.

30. "WS," *Packet*, September 9, 1779. "Statement of Charles Willson Peale," William B. Reed, *Life and Correspondence of Joseph Reed*, 2 vols. (Philadelphia, 1847), II, Appendix I, 423.

31. "C— S—," *Packet*, October 16, 1779.

32. *Ibid.*, October 2, 1779.

33. "C—S—," *Packet*, October 16, 1779.

34. James Gibson, "The Attack on Fort Wilson," *Pennsylvania Magazine of History and Biography* 5 (1881):475.

35. C—S—," *Packet*, October 16, 1779. "The Reminiscences of David Hayfield Conyngham, 1750–1834," ed. Horad Edwin Hayden, *Wyoming Historical and Geological Society, Proceedings and Collections* 8 (1904):208–10.

36. "The Address of a Number of Officers of the City Militia of Philadelphia," *Packet*, October 21, 1779. Samuel Patterson to Caesar Rodney, October 6, 1779, *Letters to and from Caesar Rodney, 1756–1784*, ed. George Herbert Ryden (Philadelphia: University of Pennsylvania Press, 1933), pp. 322–23.

37. "C—S—," *Packet*, October 16, 1779.

38. *Gazette*, October 20, 1779.

39. *Evening Post*, August 8 and 15, 1778. *A Card* (Philadelphia, October 13, 1778).

40. "To the Citizens of Pennsylvania," *Packet*, March 25, 1779.

41. *Gazette*, March 24, 1779.

42. Benjamin Rush to John Dickinson, March 20, 1778, Robert R. Logan Collection, LCP. Bray Hammond, *Banks and Politics in America, from the Revolution to the Civil War* (Princeton: Princeton University Press, 1957), pp. 60–61.

43. *To the Inhabitants of Pennsylvania* (Philadelphia, July 11, 1779).

44. Until 1779, there being no census, two representatives were alloted to each county: after 1779, representation was apportioned on the basis of the population of each county. Robert L. Brunhouse, *The Counter-Revolution in Pennsylvania, 1776–1790* (Harrisburg: Pennsylvania Historical Commission, 1942), p. 77.

45. *Gazette*, October 18, 1780.

46. Henry Laurens to John Adams, October 4, 1779, *Letters of Members of the Continental Congress*, ed. Edmund C. Burnett (Washington, D.C.: The Carnegie Institution, 1921–36), IV, 468.

47. Warner, *Private City*, p. 44.

48. Ferguson, *Power of the Purse*, pp. 122–24, 134.

49. Hammond, *Banks and Politics*, pp. 50–51. Ferguson, *Power of the Purse*, pp. 62–63.

50. *Independent Gazetteer*, April 1, 1786. See also, "A Friend to Mechanics," *Packet*, June 28, 1783.

51. *Gazette*, October 17, 1781, and October 16, 1782.

52. See, for example, "Irish Cooper," *Journal*, March 20, 1782; "A Me-

chanic," *Packet,* June 21, 1781; and "Hint," *Freeman's Journal,* December 18, 1782.

53. J. P. Brissot de Warville, *New Travels in the United States of America, 1788,* trans. Mara Soceanu Vamos and Furand Echeuerria (Cambridge, Mass.: Harvard University Press, 1964), p. 259.

54. "Jurisparitus," *Gazette,* January 29, 1783.

55. "A Friend to Mechanics," *Freeman's Journal,* June 25, 1783.

56. *Gazette,* February 20, 1782.

57. *Independent Gazetteer,* May 3, 1783.

58. *Freeman's Journal,* July 9, 1783.

59. *Independent Gazetteer,* July 19, 1783.

60. *Ibid.*

61. See, for example, "Common Sense," *Freeman's Journal,* September 24, 1783; and *Independent Gazetteer,* July 31, 1784.

62. Brunhouse, *Counter-Revolution,* pp. 134–35.

63. *The Alternative* (Philadelphia, October, 1783). "A Tradesman of Philadelphia," *Packet,* February 2, 1783.

64. *Ibid.,* May 31, 1783.

65. "A Friend to all Mechanics," *Independent Gazetteer,* October 11, 1783.

66. "A Brother Mechanic," *ibid.,* October 11, 1783.

67. *Ibid.,* October 11, 1783.

68. *Gazette,* October 22, 1783.

VIII—The Urban Coalescence, 1783–86

1. See, for example, "A Pennsylvanian," *Gazette,* August 4, 1784.

2. Robert L. Brunhouse, *The Counter-Revolution in Pennsylvania, 1776–1790* (Harrisburg: Pennsylvania Historical Commission, 1942), pp. 142–43.

3. Thomas Paine to Daniel Clymer, September, 1786, Clymer Manuscripts, HSP. "A Citizen," *Mercury,* December 10, 1784. "A Friend to both sides of the Susquehanna," *Independent Gazetteer,* December 2, 1786. "Philadelphiensis," *Freeman's Journal,* January 19, 1785.

4. Chaloner and White to ———, March 21, 1784, Chaloner and White Letter Book, HSP. "A Pennsylvanian," *Independent Gazetteeer,* December 24, 1784.

5. Hawthorn and Kerr to John Bachelor, May 14, 1785, Hawthorn and Kerr Letter Book, HSP.

6. "Candid," *Gazette,* April 6, 1785.

7. Bray Hammond, *Banks and Politics in America, from the Revolution to the Civil War* (Princeton: Princeton University Press, 1957), pp. 53–56.

8. Wilbur C. Plummer, "Consumer Credit in Colonial Philadelphia," *Pennsylvania Magazine of History and Biography* 64 (1942):390–91.

9. "Amicus," *Freeman's Journal*, December 13, 1786. See also, *Evening Herald*, February 26, 1785.

10. "Strictures on the Bank, and on a Paper Currency," *Packet*, March 31, April 1, 1785.

11. "A Mechanic," *Independent Gazetteer*, March 13, 1784.

12. Ebenezer Hazard to Jeremy Belknap, January 24, 1784, quoted in Brunhouse, *Counter-Revolution*, p. 150.

13. *Independent Gazetteer*, January 31 and February 7, 1784.

14. *Packet*, January 22, 1784.

15. "An American," *ibid.*, February 3, 1784. "To the Public," *ibid.*, March 2, 1784.

16. *Independent Gazetteer*, March 6, 1784. "Liberty," *Freeman's Journal*, March 16, 1784. "To the Public," *Packet*, March 2, 1784.

17. *Independent Gazetteer*, March 20, 1784.

18. "A Mechanic," *Mercury and Advertiser*, October 1, 1784.

19. "Querist," *Independent Gazetteer*, May 22 and July 31, 1784.

20. "A Country Freeman," *Mercury and Advertiser*, November 19, 1784. "A Planter," *Evening Herald*, August 3, 1785.

21. "A Dialogue between a Citizen of Philadelphia and a Country Assemblyman," *Independent Gazetteer*, August 14, 1784.

22. "A Son of St. Tamany," *ibid.*, May 1, 1784.

23. "A Friend to Liberty," *Packet*, October 9, 1784.

24. Brunhouse, *Counter-Revolution*, pp. 153–54.

25. "One of the Little Folk," *Evening Herald*, November 20, 1785.

26. *To the Citizens of Pennsylvania* (Philadelphia, September 29, 1784). *Packet*, October 1, 1784.

27. *Packet*, October 7, 1785.

28. *Freeman's Journal*, April 13, 1785.

29. "An Old Mechanic," *Independent Gazetteer*, October 9, 1784. "Arminius," *ibid.*

30. *Gazette*, October 20, 1784. Brunhouse, *Counter-Revolution*, p. 164.

31. "A Proposed Address from the *Representatives* of the *Freemen* of the *Commonwealth* of *Pennsylvania* . . . to their *Constituents*," *Packet*, December 27, 1784.

32. "A Message from the General Assembly," *ibid.*, December 30, 1784.

33. "A Customer," *Independent Gazetteer,* September 24 and October 1, 1785. *Evening Herald,* March 26, 1785.

34. Hammond, *Banks and Politics,* p. 53.

35. *Evening Herald,* March 22, 1785. "To the Mechanics and Manufacturers of Pennsylvania," *Independent Gazetteer,* September 16, 1786.

36. *Gazette,* April 27, 1785.

37. *Journal,* December 30, 1785.

38. *Independent Gazetteer,* August 19, 1786.

39. "Wantplace and Hold Post," *Gazette,* January 19, 1785. *Evening Herald,* February 22 and June 18, 1785.

40. "A Proposed Address from the *Representatives* of the *Freemen* of the *Commonwealth* of *Pennsylvania* . . . to their *Constituents,*" *Packet,* December 27, 1784.

41. "A Mechanic," *Independent Gazetteer,* January 8, 1785.

42. "A Constitutionalist," *Independent Gazetteer,* January 15, 1785; see also, "A Tradesman," *ibid.,* January 23, 1785.

43. "A Constitutionalist," *ibid.,* January 15, 1785.

44. "To the Public," *Evening Herald,* March 22, 1785.

45. *Ibid.*

46. *Ibid.*

47. *Packet,* May 13, 1785. The bill was transcribed in Assembly March 22, 1785; this date coincides with the meeting of cordwainers.

48. *Gazette,* July 27, 1785.

49. *Independent Gazetteer,* October 1, 1785.

50. "A Proposed Address from the *Representatives* of the *Freemen* of the *Commonwealth* of *Pennsylvania* . . . to their *Constituents,*" *Packet,* December 27, 1784. The complete statement of the radical economic program, contains no mention of tariffs.

51. Chaloner and White to Wadsworth, December 28, 1783, Chaloner and White Letter Book, HSP.

52. *Journal,* February 26, 1785.

53. "A Message from the General Assembly . . . ," *Packet,* December 30, 1784.

54. Hawthorn and Kerr to Robert Byrn, June 6, 1785, and Hawthorn and Kerr to George Lang and Company, May 26, 1785, Hawthorn and Kerr Letter Book, HSP.

55. "A Merchant of Philadelphia," *Packet,* November 11, 1784. Subsequently, merchants formed a "Commercial Committee," to act as a legislative lobby. "The Merchants of this City," *ibid.,* July 12, 1785.

56. "Pro Bono-Reipublicae," *Gazette,* May 11, 1785.

57. "Common Sense," *ibid.*

58. *Ibid.*, June 22, 1785.

59. *Ibid.* Italics in original.

60. *Evening Herald*, June 4, 1785. *Gazette*, June 22, 1785.

61. *Journal*, July 12, 1785. Tench Coxe, *An Address to the Assembly of the Friends of American Manufactures* . . . (Philadelphia, 1787). "An American," *Journal*, August 15, 1785.

62. "A Consistent American," *Evening Herald*, August 27, 1785.

63. *Packet*, October 7 and October 10, 1785. "Constitutionalists and Mechanics," *Freeman's Journal*, October 5, 1785.

64. "Mirror," *Freeman's Journal*, October 5, 1785.

65. *Ibid.*

66. "A Philadelphia Mechanic," *Independent Gazetteer*, October 3, 1785.

67. *Evening Herald*, October 5, 1785.

68. *Independent Gazetteer*, October 3, 1785, printed an erroneous list of Constitutionalist candidates, probably in an effort to confuse the opposition. The correct ticket appeared in *Packet*, October 7, 1785.

IX—Concluding the Revolution, 1786–89

1. "A Merchant," *Mercury and Advertiser*, March 3, 1786.

2. *Ibid.*, June 9, 1786.

3. "Association," *Freeman's Journal*, June 14, 1786.

4. "A Merchant," *Mercury and Advertiser*, March 3, 1786.

5. *Independent Gazetteer*, December 31, 1785. "A Citizen," *ibid.*, July 30, 1787.

6. "Nestor," *ibid.*, July 1, 1786.

7. *Ibid.*

8. "To the Mechanics and Manufacturers of Pennsylvania," *ibid.*, September 16, 1786. Italics in original.

9. *Ibid.* The motion passed by only four votes.

10. *Ibid.*

11. *Ibid.*, September 23, 1786.

12. *Ibid.*

13. *Mercury and Advertiser*, November 10, 1786.

14. *Independent Gazetteer,* November 27, 1786. *Mercury and Advertiser,* November 10, 1786.

15. *Mercury and Advertiser,* November 10, 1786.

16. *Freeman's Journal,* August 3, 1787.

17. "A Mechanic," *Independent Gazetteer,* July 20, 1787. "Raciocinator," *Gazette,* August 27, 1788.

18. George Bryan, Account of the Adoption of the Constitution of 1787, George Bryan Papers, 1785–1787, HSP.

19. "A Pennsylvanian," *Independent Gazetteer,* April 25, 1787.

20. "Curio," *ibid.,* August 22, 1787.

21. *Ibid.,* September 12, 1787.

22. "A Correspondent," *ibid.,* August 4, 1787.

23. *Ibid.,* September 21, 1787.

24. "A Real Friend to American Manufactures," *Freeman's Journal,* September 12, 1787.

25. "Report of the Managers of the Pennsylvania Society for the Encouragement of American Manufactures and useful Arts," *Independent Gazetteer,* February 11, 1788.

26. "A Pennsylvanian," *ibid.,* April 4, 1787.

27. Edmund S. Morgan, "The Political Establishments of the United States, 1784," *William and Mary Quarterly,* 3rd Series, 23 (1966):286–87.

28. "A Federalist," *Independent Gazetteer,* October 10, 1787, indicated that the labels "Federalist," and "Antifederalist" had supplanted "Republican" and "Constitutionalist" by the autumn of 1787. The change of name did not alter the political content of the two parties.

29. The consensus did not, of course, extend outside Philadelphia. There was substantial opposition to the Constitution in the Pennsylvania back country, which was only overcome by careful political engineering, and some chicanery, in the Pennsylvania ratifying convention.

30. *Gazette,* January 23, 1788.

31. Bryan, Account of the Adoption of the Constitution, Bryan Papers, HSP. "A Citizen," *Gazette,* April 2, 1788, corroborated Bryan.

32. Bryan, Account of the Adoption of the Constitution, Bryan Papers, HSP.

33. *Ibid.*

34. *Ibid.*

35. "A Mechanic," *Independent Gazetteer,* April 23, 1788.

36. "A Bricklayer," *ibid.,* February 15, 1788.

37. "A Pennsylvanian," *Freeman's Journal,* January 30, 1788.

38. Bryan, Account of the Adoption of the Constitution, Bryan Papers, HSP.

39. *Independent Gazetteer,* October 11, 1787.

40. *Journal,* November 10, 1787.

41. Bryan, Account of the Adoption of the Constitution, Bryan Papers, HSP.

42. *Minutes of the Convention of Pennsylvania &c.* (Philadelphia, 1787).

43. Francis Hopkinson, *An Account of the Grand Federal Procession . . . ,* (Philadelphia, 1788).

44. *Freeman's Journal,* April 1, 1789.

45. See, for example, stories in the news columns of *Gazette,* September 24; October 1, 15, 29; November 5; December 24, 1788; and April 1, 1789.

46. *Ibid.,* February 18, 1789.

47. "An American Citizen," *ibid.,* October 29, 1788.

48. See, for example, *ibid.,* February 20, and June 25, 1788.

49. *Ibid.,* June 25, 1788.

50. *Ibid.,* November 26, 1788.

51. *Ibid.,* December 3 and 24, 1788.

52. *Freeman's Journal,* August 23, 1786. *Journal,* February 4, 1789.

53. *Gazette,* March 18, 1789.

54. *Ibid.,* March 11 and 18, 1789.

55. *The Constitution and Ordinances of the City of Philadelphia, Extracts from the Minutes of the Corporation* (Philadelphia, 1790). *Gazette,* April 15 and 22, 1789.

56. *State of Pennsylvania in General Assembly* (Philadelphia, 1789).

57. Examples of this propaganda appear in *Gazette,* March 11 and 25, and April 1 and 29, 1789.

58. *Minutes of the Convention of the Commonwealth of Pennsylvania* (Philadelphia, 1789). No Philadelphia mechanics attended the convention as representatives for the city.

59. *The Constitution of the Commonwealth of Pennsylvania* (Philadelphia, 1790).

ঔৈঔৈঔৈঔৈঔৈঔৈঔৈঔৈঔৈঔৈৈৈৈৈৈৈৈৈৈৈ

Bibliography

PRIMARY SOURCES

Ledgers, Accounts, Business Records

The manuscript sources on the business activities of Philadelphia's eighteenth-century mechanics are extremely rare. Artisans tended not to keep extensive records, and most that were kept have since disappeared. The few extant mechanic business records, and some merchant accounts, contain small pieces of a very large puzzle.

David Hall Day Book, Winterthur Museum.
Miers Fisher Ledger, HSP.
Richard Mason and Parnell Gibbs Day Book, HSP.
Jonathan Meredith Account of Hides Purchased, 1784–87, HSP.
Jonathan Meredith Shop Book, 1785–88, HSP.
Ledger of James Muir, 1782–95, HSP.
Stephen Paschall Ledger C, HSP.
Imports and Exports, 1771–72, to and from the Several Ports in America, Records of the Board of Commissioners for Trade and Plantations, HSP (photostat).

Letter Books

Artisans were no better correspondents than they were record-keepers. A few of the more successful and literate—William Bradford, for example—left correspondence, but they were rare exceptions. Merchant Letter Books and Correspondence, however, are often highly revealing of mechanic affairs, for many merchants had political and business dealings with tradesmen which they discussed in their writings.

William Barrel Letters, Stephen Collins Papers, XIII, XV, LC.
Owen Biddle Letter Book, January, 1780–July, 1781, Friends Historical Library, Swarthmore, Pennsylvania.
Owen Biddle Letter Book, 1771, Friends Historical Library, Swarthmore, Pennsylvania.
William Bradford Correspondence, HSP.
Chaloner and White Letter Book, HSP.
Thomas Clifford Correspondence, HSP.
Thomas Clifford Letter Book, 1759–66, HSP.
Thomas Clifford Letter Book, 1767–73, HSP.
Samuel Coates Letter Book, HSP.
Henry Drinker Letter Book, 1772–86, HSP.
Hawthorn and Kerr Letter Book, HSP.
Joshua Humphreys Letter Book, HSP.
Orr, Dunlope & Glenholme Letter Book, HSP.
John Reynell Letter Book, May, 1769–November, 1770, HSP.
John Reynell Letter Book, 1770, HSP.
Thomas Wharton Letter Book, 1773–84, HSP.

Guilds, Fire Companies, Social Organizations

Historians have long noted that Philadelphia was a city over-run with social organizations of various kinds and characters. The mechanics of the revolutionary period were on the move socially, and their participation in social organizations was therefore quite extensive. The richest manuscript resources on these societies are:

The Carpenters Company Wardens Book, 1769–81, APS.
Minutes of the Cordwainers Fire Company, HSP.
Minutes of the Friendship Carpenters Company, 1769–75, APS.
Minutes of the Transactions of the Taylors Company of Philadelphia, HSP.
Ledger of the Hibernia Fire Company, HSP.
Ledger Belonging to the Delaware Fire Company, HSP.
Minute Book of the Delaware Fire Company, HSP.
Minutes of the Union Fire Company, Commencing the 7th Day of December, 1736, 2 volumes, LCP.
Society of the Sons of St. George, Minutes, HSP.
Register of the Jockey Club, HSP.
Mount Regale Fishing Company Papers, HSP.

Other Manuscript Sources

The Historical Society of Pennsylvania and the Library Company of Philadelphia have many scores of manuscript and manuscript collections on eighteenth-century Philadelphia which must be carefully perused by serious students of the city's social history. Among the most useful for the study of mechanics were the following.

George Bryan Papers, 1785–87, HSP.
Daniel Clymer Manuscripts, HSP.
John Dickinson Papers, HSP.
Joshua and Thomas Fisher Papers, HSP.
Robert R. Logan Collection, LCP.
Du Simitière Papers, LCP.
William Smith Manuscripts, 1765–74, HSP.
Charles Thomson Memorandum Book, 1754–74, HSP.
A Catalogue of Books belonging to the Association Library Company of Philadelphia, HSP.
Manuscript Declaration of Philadelphia Coopers, 1742, HSP.
Tax List, 1769, HSP.
Tax List, 1774, HSP.

Published Manuscripts and Manuscript Collections

Many of the very best manuscript sources of the Historical Society of Pennsylvania and other repositories have been reproduced in print. Wherever possible, the original manuscripts were consulted for this book on the mechanics, but the printed versions (often edited and abridged, but seldom altered substantially) are cited in the notes and bibliography for the convenience of other students.

Letters and Correspondence

Letters of Members of the Continental Congress, ed. Edmund C. Burnett, 8 volumes (Washington, D.C.: Carnegie Institution, 1921–36).
Papers of Benjamin Franklin, ed. Leonard W. Labaree, 14 volumes, to date (New Haven: Yale University Press, 1959–70).
The Correspondence of General Thomas Gage with the Secretaries of State, 1763–1775, ed. Clarence E. Carter, 2 volumes (New Haven: Yale University Press, 1931–33).
The Complete Writings of Thomas Paine, ed. Philip S. Foner, 2 volumes (New York: The Citadel Press, 1945).
Letters to and from Caesar Rodney, 1756–1784, ed. George Herbert Ryden (Philadelphia: University of Pennsylvania Press, 1933).
Letters of Benjamin Rush, ed. Lyman H. Butterfield, 2 volumes (Princeton: Princeton University Press, 1951), I.

Diaries, Journals, Brief Accounts

John Adams, *Diary, The Adams Papers,* 1st Series, ed. Lyman H. Butterfield, 4 volumes (Cambridge, Mass.: Harvard University Press, 1961).
"Extracts from the Diary of Dr. James Clitherall, 1776," *Pennsylvania Magazine of History and Biography* 22 (1878):468–74.
"The Reminiscences of David Hayfield Conyngham, 1750–1834," ed. Horad Edwin Hayden, *Wyoming Historical and Geological Society, Proceedings and Collections* 8 (1904):208–15.
Extracts from the Journal of Elizabeth Drinker, ed. Henry D. Biddle (Philadelphia, 1889).
"Journal of Samuel Rowland Fisher, of Philadelphia, 1779–1781," ed. Anna Wharton Morris, *Pennsylvania Magazine of History and Biography* 41 (1917):145–97, 274–333, and 399–457.
Extracts from the Diary of Jacob Hiltzheimer, ed. Jacob Cox Parsons (Philadelphia, 1893).
Extracts from the Diary of Christopher Marshall, Kept in Philadelphia and Lancaster During the American Revolution, 1776–1781, ed. William Duane (Albany, N.Y., 1877).

Life and Correspondence of Joseph Reed, ed. William B. Reed, 2 volumes (Philadelphia, 1847).

Other Manuscripts and Collections

American Archives, 4th series, ed. Peter Force, 3 volumes (Washington, D.C., 1837).

George Cuthbert to Lieutenant-General John Dalling, April, 1775, *Pennsylvania Magazine of History and Biography* 66 (1942):206–15.

Silas Deane to Simeon Deane, 1779, *Pennsylvania Magazine of History and Biography* 17 (1893):348–51.

"The Effects of the 'Non-Importation Agreement' in Philadelphia, 1769–1770" [letters of Henry Drinker], *Pennsylvania Magazine of History and Biography* 14 (1891):41–45.

James Gibson, "The Attack on Fort Wilson," *Pennsylvania Magazine of History and Biography* 5 (1881):475–76.

"The Thomson Papers," *Collections of the New York Historical Society* 11 (1878).

PRINTED SOURCES

Newspapers

Newspapers are indisputably the most important sources for eighteenth-century urban social history. For this study, they provided an almost limitless mine of information about the mechanics—their names, addresses, trades, business problems, marketing aspirations, competitive frustrations, and a wealth of other data are contained in the scores of mechanic advertisements which sprinkle every issue. The newspapers contain accounts of the major public events in the city—town meetings, and the like—though these must be read carefully and in conjunction with other sources, since printers presumed rumor and gossip would convey much to readers that is not available to historians. Finally, the newspapers contain a wealth of opinion by and about mechanics, expressed by editors and a long stream of correspondents. Every issue of every extant Philadephia newspaper, 1765–90, was examined for this study. All are available on microfilm. (Dates given in parentheses indicate the period of time during which the paper was published; for newspapers whose publishing runs began before or ended after the Revolutionary era, the beginning and terminal dates are given as 1765 or 1790. Citations in the notes of this book refer to the newspapers by short title.)

The Freeman's Journal: or, the North-American Intelligencer (1781–90).
The Independent Gazetteer; or, the Chronicle of Freedom (1782–90).
The Pennsylvania Chronicle and Universal Advertiser (1767–74).
The Pennsylvania Evening Herald and The American Monitor (1785–88).
The Pennsylvania Evening Post and General Advertiser (1775–79).
The Pennsylvania Gazette (1765–90).
The Pennsylvania Journal and Weekly Advertiser (1765–90).
The Pennsylvania Mercury and Universal Advertiser (1784–90).
The Pennsylvania Packet, and Daily Advertiser (1771–90).
Story and Humphrey's Pennsylvania Mercury and Universal Advertiser (1775).

Government Documents

The several series of the *Pennsylvania Archives and Pennsylvania Colonial Records* and other published government documents contain information essential to political history. The most useful for the study of mechanics are the following:

The Acts of Assembly of the Province of Pennsylvania; Carefully Compared with the Originals (Philadelphia, 1775).
The Constitution o fthe Commonwealth of Pennsylvania (Philadelphia, 1776).
The Constitution of the Commonwealth of Pennsylvania (Philadelphia, 1790).
Minutes of the Common Council of the City of Philadelphia, 1704–1776 (Philadelphia, 1847).
Minutes of the Convention of the Commonwealth of Pennsylvania (Philadelphia, 1789).
Minutes of the Convention of Pennsylvania (Philadelphia, 1787).
The Minutes of the Provincial Council of Pennsylvania, Pennsylvania Colonial Records, 14 volumes (Harrisburg, 1852), 9–10.
Votes and Proceedings of the House of Representatives of the Province of Pennsylvania, Pennsylvania Archives, 8th series, 8 volumes (Harrisburg, 1935), 6–8.

Broadsides and Other Contemporary Printed Sources

Philadelphia had a good many printing presses in the latter part of the eighteenth century, and they were kept busy by the citizenry. It is the good fortune of historians that nearly all the extant printed material is now readily available in the Early American Imprint Series of the American Antiquarian Society.

Broadsides (*listed chronologically*)

David Hall, *Lately Imported, and to be Sold by David Hall* (Philadelphia, 1765).

James Biddle, *To the Freeholders and Electors of the Province of Pennsylvania* (Philadelphia, 1765).

[John Dickinson], *The Late Regulations Respecting the British Colonies* (Philadelphia, 1765).

John Morgan, *Dissertation on the Reciprocal Advantages of a Perpetual Union between Great-Britain and her American Colonies* (Philadelphia, 1766).

The Following Address Was Read at a Meeting of the Merchants, at the Lodge in Philadelphia, on Monday, the 25th of April, 1768 (Philadelphia, 1768).

John Dickinson, *Letters from a Farmer in Pennsylvania to the Inhabitants of the British Colonies* (New York, 1768).

William Bradford, *Imported in the Last Vessels from London* (Philadelphia, 1769).

To the Free and Patriotic Inhabitants of the City of Philad. and Province of Pennsylvania (Philadelphia, May 31, 1770).

To the Tradesmen, Farmers, and other Inhabitants of the City and County of Philadelphia (Philadelphia, September 24, 1770).

To the Freeholders, Merchants, Tradesmen and Farmers of the City and County of Philad. (Philadelphia, September 26, 1770).

Philadelphia, Thursday, September 27, 1770. Many Respectable Freeholders . . . (Philadelphia, September 27, 1770).

To the Worthy Tradesmen, Artificers, Mechanics &c. Electors for the City and County of Philadelphia (Philadelphia, October 1, 1770).

Fellow Citizens and Countrymen (Philadelphia, October 1, 1770).

To the Public (Philadelphia, October 3, 1770).

From the Merchants and Traders of Philadelphia . . . to the Merchants and Manufacturers of Great Britain (Philadelphia, 1770).

The Partnership; or the History of the Rise and Progress of the Pennsylvania Chronicle (Philadelphia, 1770).

Transactions of the American Philosophical Society, Held at Philadelphia, for Promoting useful Knowledge (Philadelphia, 1771).

A Tradesman's Address to his Countrymen (Philadelphia, March 2, 1772).

To the Freemen of Pennsylvania (Philadelphia, 1772).

A Card (Philadelphia, December 2, 1773).

To the Manufacturers and Mechanics of Philadelphia, the Northern Liberties, and District of Southwark (Philadelphia, June 8, 1774).

At a Meeting at the Philosophical Society's Hall (Philadelphia, June 10, 1774).

Philadelphia, May 20 (Philadelphia, May 20, 1776).

At a Meeting Held at the Philosophical Society Hall . . . (Philadelphia, October 17, 1776).

To the Freeholders and Independent Electors of Philadelphia (Philadelphia, November 5, 1776).

At a Meeting of a Number of Citizens of Philadelphia at the Philosophical Society Hall . . . (Philadelphia, November 8, 1776).

The Constitution of the Commonwealth of Pennsylvania (Philadelphia, 1776).

Proceedings of the Provincial Conference of Committees of the Province of Pennsylvania (Philadelphia, 1776).

To the People (Philadelphia, 1776).

A Card (Philadelphia, October 13, 1778).

At a General Meeting of the Citizens of Philadelphia and Parts Adjacent . . . (Philadelphia, May 25, 1779).

To the Inhabitants of Pennsylvania (Philadelphia, July 1, 1779).

The Independent and Constitutional Ticket (Philadelphia, [1779]).

The Alternative (Philadelphia, October, 1783).

To the Citizens of Pennsylvania (Philadelphia, September 29, 1784).

An Address of the Council of Censors to the Freemen of Pennsylvania (Philadelphia, 1784).

[James Wilson], *Considerations on the Bank of North-America* (Philadelphia, 1785).

David MacBride, *An Improved Method of Tanning Leather* (Philadelphia, 1786; originally published in Dublin, 1785).

Remarks on a Pamphlet Entitled, 'Considerations on the Bank of North-America' (Philadelphia, 1785).

Tench Coxe, *An Address to the Assembly of the Friends of American Manufactures . . .* (Philadelphia, 1787).

Francis Hopkinson, *Account of the Grand Federal Procession . . .* (Philadelphia, 1788).

Act to Incorporate the City of Philadelphia (Philadelphia, 1789).

State of Pennsylvania in General Assembly (Philadelphia, 1789).
The Constitution and Ordinances of Philadelphia, Extracts from the Minutes of the Corporation (Philadelphia, 1790).

Longer Printed Works

Articles of the Carpenters Company of Philadelphia, and their Rules for Measuring and Valuing House-Carpenters Work (Philadelphia, 1786).
Francis White, *The Philadelphia Directory* (Philadelphia, 1785).
The Constitution and Rules of the St. Andrews Society in Philadelphia (Philadelphia, 1769).
An Historical Catelogue of the St. Andrews Society of Philadelphia, 1749–1781 (Philadelphia, 1782).
J. P. Brissot de Warville, *New Travels in the United States of America, 1788,* trans. Mara Soceanu Vamos and Furand Echeuerria (Cambridge, Mass.: Harvard University Press, 1964).
Alexander Graydon, *Memoirs of His Own Times with Reminiscences of Men and Events,* ed. John S. Littell (Philadelphia, 1846).
"Patrick M'Robert's *Tour through Part of the Northern Provinces of America,*" ed. Carl Bridenbaugh, *Pennsylvania Magazine of History and Biography* 59(1935):134–80.

SECONDARY SOURCES

The historical literature on the American Revolution in general, and on Pennsylvania and Philadelphia in particular, is extensive. Aside from a few studies of mechanics in other cities, however, there is little which bears directly on the artisans. The books and articles cited here and in the notes were used primarily as sources of information on issues, problems, controversies, and occurrences which are related to the story of the mechanics yet not of such importance as to warrant re-study. Secondarily, the literature was used as general background, and thus a few works appear here which are not cited in the notes.

Books

Allison, Edward P. and Boies Penrose, *Philadelphia, 1681–1887: A History of Municipal Development* (Philadelphia: 1887).

Andrews, Charles M., *The Colonial Period of American History*, 4 volumes (New Haven: Yale University Press, 1934), 4.

Beard, Charles A., *The Economic Interpretation of the Constitution of the United States* (New York: 1913).

Becker, Carl L., *The History of Political Parties in the Province of New York, 1760–1776* (Madison, Wisc.: 1909).

Benson, Lee, *Turner and Beard; American Historical Writing Reconsidered* (Glencoe, Ill.: Free Press, 1960).

Bezanson, Anne, *Prices and Inflation During the American Revolution; Pennsylvania, 1770–1790* (Philadelphia: University of Pennsylvania Press, 1951).

Bining, Aruthur C., *British Regulation of the Colonial Iron Industry* (Philadelphia: University of Pennsylvania Press, 1933).

Bjerko, Ethel Hall, *The Cabinet Makers of America* (Garden City, N.J.: Doubleday, 1957).

Bridenbaugh, Carl, *Cities in Revolt; Urban Life in America, 1743–1776* (New York: Knopf, 1955).

———, *Cities in the Wilderness; The First Century of Urban Life in America, 1625–1742* (New York: Knopf, 1955).

———, *The Colonial Craftsman* (New York: New York University Press, 1950).

———, and Bridenbaugh, Jessica, *Rebels and Gentlemen; Philadelphia in the Age of Franklin* (New York: Reynal and Hitchcock, 1942).

Brown, Robert E., *Charles Beard and the Economic Interpretation of the Constitution of the United States* (Princeton: Princeton University Press, 1956).

———, *Middle-Class Democracy and the Revolution in Massachusetts, 1691–1780* (Ithaca, N.Y.: Cornell University Press, 1955).

Brunhouse, Robert L., *The Counter-Revolution in Pennsylvania, 1776–1790* (Harrisburg, Pa.: Pennsylvania Historical Commission, 1942).

Cambridge Economic History of Europe, III: Economic Organization and Policies in the Middle Ages (Cambridge: At the University Press, 1963).

Clark, Victor S., *History of Manufacturing in the United States, 1607–1860* (Washington, D.C., 1916).

Cunningham, William, *The Growth of English Industry and Commerce During the Early Middle Ages* (Cambridge, 1910).

Dewey, Davis Rich, *Financial History of the United States* (New York, 1903).

East, Robert A., *Business Enterprise in the American Revolutionary Era* (New York: Columbia University Press, 1938).

Eckhardt, George H., *Pennsylvania Clocks and Clockmakers* (New York: Devin-Adair, 1955).

Ferguson, E. James, *The Power of the Purse: A History of American Public Finance, 1776–1790* (Chapel Hill: University of North Carolina Press, 1961).

Hammond, Bray, *Banks and Politics in America from the Revolution to the Civil War* (Princeton: Princeton University Press, 1957).

Hanna, William S., *Benjamin Franklin and Pennsylvania Politics* (Stanford: Stanford University Press, 1964).

Hawke, David, *In the Midst of a Revolution* (Philadelphia: University of Pennsylvania Press, 1961).

Hindle, Brooke, *David Rittenhouse* (Princeton: Princeton University Press, 1964).

————, *The Pursuit of Science in Revolutionary America, 1735–1789* (Chapel Hill: University of North Carolina Press, 1956).

Hutson, James H., *Pennsylvania Politics, 1746–1776: the Movement for Royal Government and Its Consequences* (Princeton: Princeton University Press, 1972).

Jackson, Joseph, *Market Street, Philadelphia; the Most Historic Highway in America; Its Merchants and Its Story* (Philadelphia, 1918).

Jacobson, David L., *John Dickinson and the Revolution in Pennsylvania* (Berkeley and Los Angeles: University of California Press, 1965).

Jameson, J. Franklin, *The American Revolution Considered as a Social Movement* (Princeton: Princeton University Press, 1926).

Jensen, Arthur, *The Maritime Commerce of Colonial Philadelphia* (Madison, Wis.: University of Wisconsin Press, 1963).

Jensen, Merrill, *The New Nation; a History of the United States During the Confederation, 1781–1789* (New York: Knopf, 1950).

Konkle, Burton Alva, *George Bryan and the Constitution of Pennsylvania, 1731–1791* (Philadelphia: W. S. Campbell, 1922).

————, *Thomas Willing and the First American Financial System* (Philadelphia: University of Pennsylvania Press, 1937).

Lincoln, Charles H., *The Revolutionary Movement in Pennsylvania* (Philadelphia, 1901).

Lipson, Ephraim, *The Economic History of England*, 3 volumes (London: A. & C. Black, Ltd., 1929), I [*The Middle Ages*].

Maier, Pauline, *From Resistance to Revolution: Colonial Radicals and the Development of American Oppostion to Britain, 1765–1776* (New York: Random House, 1974).

Main, Jackson T., *The Social Structure of Revolutionary America* (Princeton: Princeton University Press, 1965).

McDonald, Forrest, *E. Pluribus Unum; the Formation of the American Republic 1776–1790* (Boston: Houghton Mifflin, 1965).

————, *We, the People: the Economic Origins of the Constitution* (Chicago: University of Chicago Press, 1958).

McKearin, George S. and Helen M., *American Glass* (New York: Crown, 1941).

Miner, Ward L., *William Goddard, Newspaperman* (Durham, N.C.: Duke University Press, 1962).

Morgan, Edmund S. and Helen M., *The Stamp Act Crisis; Prologue to Revolution* (Chapel Hill: University of North Carolina Press, 1953).

Morris, Richard, *The American Revolution Reconsidered* (New York: Harper and Row, 1968).

————, *Government and Labor in Early America* (New York: Columbia University Press, 1942).

Pares, Richard, *Yankees and Creoles* (Cambridge, Mass.: Harvard University Press, 1956).

Ramsay, John, *American Potters and Pottery* (Boston: Houghton Mifflin, 1959).

Rossman, Kenneth R., *Thomas Mifflin and the Politics of the American Revolution* (Chapel Hill: University of North Carolina Press, 1952).

Savelle, Max, *George Morgan, Colony Builder* (New York: Columbia University Press, 1932).

Scharf, J. Thomas and Wescott, Thompson, *History of Philadelphia, 1609–1884,* 3 volumes (Philadelphia: 1884), I.

Schlesinger, Arthur, *The Colonial Merchants and the American Revolution* (New York: 1917).

Selsam, J. Paul, *The Pennsylvania Constitution of 1776* (Philadelphia: University of Pennsylvania Press, 1936).

Sharpless, Isaac, *Political Leaders of Provincial Pennsylvania* (New York: Macmillan, 1919).

Smart, Charles E., *The Makers of Surveying Instruments in America Since 1700* (Troy, N.Y.: Regal Arts Press, 1962).

Smith, Abbot E., *Colonists in Bondage: White Servitude and Convict Labor in Early America, 1607–1776* (Chapel Hill: University of North Carolina Press, 1947).

Thayer, Theodore, *Pennsylvania Politics and the Growth of Democracy, 1740–1776* (Harrisburg: Pennsylvania Historical and Museum Commission, 1953).

Walsh, Richard, *Charleston's Sons of Liberty: A Study of the Artisans, 1763–1789* (Columbia, S.C.: University of South Carolina Press, 1959).

Warner, Sam Bass, *The Private City; Philadelphia in Three Periods of Its Growth* (Philadelphia: University of Pennsylvania Press, 1968).

Watson, John F., *Annals of Philadelphia in the Olden Time,* 3 volumes (Philadelphia: 1899).

Williamson, Chilton, *American Suffrage: From Property to Democracy* (Princeton: Princeton University Press, 1960).

Articles

Berg, Harry D., "The Organization of Business in Colonial Philadelphia," *Pennsylvania History* 10 (1943):157–77.

Biddle, Henry D., "Owen Biddle," *Pennsylvania Magazine of History and Biography* 16 (1892):299–329.

Brunhouse, Robert L., "The Effects of the Townshend Acts in Pennsylvania," *Pennsylvania Magazine of History and Biography* 54 (1930):355–73.

Cabeen, Francis Von A., "The Society of the Sons of St. Tammany of Philadelphia," *Pennsylvania Magazine of History and Biography* 25 (1901):433–51.

Diamondstone, Judith M., "Philadelphia's Municipal Corporation, 1701–1776," *Pennsylvania Magazine of History and Biography* 90 (1966): 183–201.

Gillingham, Harrold E., "The Philadelphia Windsor Chair and Its Journeyings," *Pennsylvania Magazine of History and Biography* 55 (1931): 301–32.

Henretta, James A., "Economic Development and Social Structure in Colonial Boston," *William and Mary Quarterly*, 3rd Series, 22 (1965):75–92.

Hutson, James H., "An Investigation of the Inarticulate: Philadelphia's White Oaks," *William and Mary Quarterly*, 3rd Series, 28 (1971):3–25.

Lamberton, E. V., "Colonial Libraries of Pennsylvania," *Pennsylvania Magazine of History and Biography* 42 (1918):193–234.

Lemisch, Jesse, "The American Revolution Seen from the Bottom Up," *Towards a New Past: Dissenting Essays in American History*, ed. Barton J. Bernstein (New York: Pantheon, 1968), ch. I.

————, "Jack Tar in the Streets: Merchant Seamen in the Politics of Revolutionary America," *William and Mary Quarterly*, 3rd Series, 25 (1968): 371–407.

————, "Listening to the 'Inarticulate': William Widger's Dream and the Loyalties of American Revolutionary Seamen in British Prisons," *Journal of Social History* 3 (1969):1–29.

————, and Alexander, John K., "The White Oaks, Jack Tar, and the Concept of the 'Inarticulate,' " *William and Mary Quarterly*, 3rd Series, 29 (1972):109–42.

Lemon, James T., "Urbanization and the Development of Eighteenth Century Southeastern Pennsylvania and Adjacent Delaware," *William and Mary Quarterly*, 3rd Series, 24 (1967):501–42.

Lynd, Staughton, "The Mechanics in New York Politics," *Class Conflict, Slavery, and the United States Constitution* (New York: Bobbs-Merrill, 1967), Ch. I.

Maier, Pauline, "The Charleston Mob and the Evolution of Popular Politics in Revolutionary South Carolina, 1765–1784," *Perspectives in American History*, IV, eds. Bernard Bailyn and Donald Fleming (Cambridge, Mass.: Harvard University Press, 1970).

———, "Popular Uprisings and Civil Authority in Eighteenth-Century America," *William and Mary Quarterly*, 3rd Series, 27 (1970): 3–35.

Meader, Lewis H., "The Council of Censors," *Pennsylvania Magazine of History and Biography* 22 (1878):265–300.

Newcomb, Benjamin, "Effects of the Stamp Act in Colonial Pennsylvania Politics," *William and Mary Quarterly*, 3rd Series, 23 (1966):257–72.

Olton, Charles S., "Philadelphia's First Environmental Crisis," *Pennsylvania Magazine of History and Biography* 98 (1974):90–100.

———, "Philadelphia's Mechanics in the First Decade of Revolution, 1765–1775," *Journal of American History* 59 (1972):311–26.

Plummer, Wilbur C., "Consumer Credit in Colonial Philidelphia," *Pennsylvania Magazine of History and Biography* 66 (1942):385–409.

Schesinger, Arthur H., "The American Revolution Reconsidered," *Political Science Quarterly* 34 (1919):61–78.

Sosin, Jack M., "Imperial Regulation of Colonial Paper Money, 1764–1773," *Pennsylvania Magazine of History and Biography* 88 (1964):174–98.

Stone, Frederick D., "Philadelphia Society One Hundred Years Ago, or the Reign of Continental Money," *Pennsylvania Magazine of History and Biography* 3 (1879):361–94.

Zimmerman, John J., "Charles Thomson, 'the Sam Adams of Philadelphia,'" *Mississippi Valley Historical Review* 45 (1958): 464–80.

———, "Benjamin Franklin and the Pennsylvania *Chronicle*," *Pennsylvania Magazine of History and Biography* 81 (1957).

Unpublished Materials

Castrodale, Anne, "Daniel Trotter, Philadelphia Craftsman," M.A. thesis, Winterthur Museum, 1962.

Clark, Raymond B., "Jonathan Gostolowe (1744–1795), Philadelphia Cabinet Maker," master's thesis, Winterthur Museum, 1956.

Duvall, R. Fenton, "Philadelphia Maritime Commerce with the British Empire, 1783–1789," Ph.D. dissertation, University of Pennsylvania, 1960.

Gandy, Martha Lou, "Joseph Richardson, Quaker Silversmith," M.A. thesis, Winterthur Museum, 1954.

Goyne, Nancy Ann, "Furniture Craftsmen in Philadelphia, 1760–1780," M.A. thesis, Winterthur Museum, 1963.

Lynd, Staughton, "The Revolution and the Common Man; Farm Tenants and Artisans in New York Politics, 1777–1788," Ph.D. dissertation, Columbia University, 1962.

Olton, Charles S., "Philadelphia Artisans and the American Revolution," Ph.D. dissertation, University of California at Berkeley, 1968.

Quimby, Ian M. G., "Apprenticeship in Colonial Philadelphia," master's thesis, Winterthur Museum, 1963.

Ryerson, Richard A., "Leadership in Crisis; Radical Committees of Philadelphia and the Coming of the Revolution in Pennsylvania, 1765–1776: A Study of Revolutionary Process," Ph.D. dissertation, The Johns Hopkins University, 1972.

Index

ARTISANS FOR INDEPENDENCE
Philadelphia Mechanics and the American Revolution

was composed in 11-point Linotype Times Roman, leaded two points
with display type in Ludlow Times New Roman, and printed letterpress
on 55-pound Perkins & Squier Special Book
by York Composition, Inc., York Pennsylvania;
adhesive bound in Columbia Triton over boards
by Vail-Ballou Press, Inc., Binghamton, New York;
and published by

SYRACUSE UNIVERSITY PRESS
Syracuse, New York 13210